Untangling Some Knots
in K–8 Writing Instruction

Shelley Peterson

Ontario Institute for Studies in Education
University of Toronto
Toronto, Ontario, Canada

EDITOR

INTERNATIONAL
Reading Association
800 BARKSDALE ROAD, PO BOX 8139
NEWARK, DE 19714-8139, USA
www.reading.org

The International Reading Association attempts, through its publications, to provide a forum for a wide spectrum of opinions on reading. This policy permits divergent viewpoints without implying the endorsement of the Association.

Director of Publications   Joan M. Irwin
Editorial Director, Books and Special Projects   Matthew W. Baker
Production Editor   Shannon Benner
Permissions Editor   Janet S. Parrack
Acquisitions and Communications Coordinator   Corinne M. Mooney
Associate Editor, Books and Special Projects   Sara J. Murphy
Assistant Editor   Charlene M. Nichols
Administrative Assistant   Michele Jester
Senior Editorial Assistant   Tyanna L. Collins
Production Department Manager   Iona Sauscermen
Supervisor, Electronic Publishing   Anette Schütz
Senior Electronic Publishing Specialist   Cheryl J. Strum
Electronic Publishing Specialist   R. Lynn Harrison
Proofreader   Elizabeth C. Hunt

Project Editors   Shannon Benner and Charlene M. Nichols

Cover Design   Linda Steere

Web addresses in this book were correct as of the publication date but may have become inactive or otherwise modified since that time. If you notice a deactivated or changed Web address, please e-mail books@reading.org with the words "Website Update" in the subject line. In your message, specify the Web link, the book title, and the page number on which the link appears.

Library of Congress Cataloging-in-Publication Data
Untangling some knots in K-8 writing instruction / Shelley Peterson, editor.
      p. cm.
Includes bibliographical references and index.
   ISBN 0-87207-513-3
   1. English language--Composition and exercises--Study and teaching (Elementary) 2. Creative writing (Elementary education) I. Peterson, Shelley.
   LB1576.U57 2003
   372.62'3--dc21
                                                                    2003009925

Contents

Acknowledgments   v

Contributors   vi

Introduction   1
SHELLEY PETERSON

Section I: Students' and Teachers' Learning Processes   5

CHAPTER 1
Untangling Approaches to Teaching Writing:
A Process of Change in One Classroom   6
PAMELA E. VAN NEST

CHAPTER 2
Untangling Knots Through Talking About Writing   17
JEANNE M. ARNOLD AND SHELLEY PETERSON

CHAPTER 3
Multiage Author Groups: One Way to Untangle
the Revision Knot   27
CATHY BRUCE

CHAPTER 4
Untangling Knots in Early Writing: Young Children's
Conceptions of Print   40
JANETTE PELLETIER AND JENNIFER LASENBY

Section II: Diversity and Teaching Writing   51

CHAPTER 5
A Complex Tangle: Teaching Writing to English Language Learners
in the Mainstream Classroom   52
MONIKA SMITH AND DONALD S. QI

CHAPTER 6
Untangling Second Language Writers' and Teachers' Knots
With Reformulation   66
SHARON LAPKIN

CHAPTER 7
A Tightly Tangled Knot: The Influence of Teachers' Gender
Perceptions on Their Assessment of Student Writing   77
SHELLEY PETERSON

Section III: Teaching Writing Using Multimedia
and the Arts   87

CHAPTER 8
Untying the Knot of Time Constraints: Using Technology
to Extend Student Writing Beyond the Classroom   88
JOSEPH ALLIN

CHAPTER 9
Unraveling the Fear of Poetry/Reveling in the Pleasure
of Poetry   96
CARL LEGGO

CHAPTER 10
The Tangle of Context: Making Meaning by Writing in Role   108
DAVID BOOTH

CHAPTER 11
Engaging Reluctant Adolescent Writers With Contemporary
Literacy: Untangling Two Knots   118
JILL KEDERSHA MCCLAY

Conclusions: Two Ways to Look at Knots   129
SHELLEY PETERSON

Author Index   131

Subject Index   134

Acknowledgments

I am grateful to the teachers, students, and researchers who created the thoughtful and beautifully written chapters in this book. They placed their faith in my idea for a book and put their creative energies into writing their chapters at a time when I could not guarantee that the book would be published. I have truly enjoyed working with all the contributors and thank them for their inspiration and hard work.

Faith is also a component in my relationship with a second group of people I want to acknowledge. This book began as a collection of action research papers written by a number of students in my first graduate course at the Peterborough campus of the Ontario Institute for Studies in Education of the University of Toronto, Canada. I thank all the students who initially contributed and who read each other's drafts and provided feedback. Some students' chapters are not in this book because they related to secondary and postsecondary classrooms. Yet, their faith in the potential of this book has helped a kernel of an idea blossom into a book that is already reaching far beyond the classroom walls where it began.

Contributors

Joseph Allin, former Associate Director of Education with the York Region Board of Education—one of Canada's largest school districts—recently retired from a 35-year career in public education during which he served as teacher, principal, and school superintendent. Currently his attention is focused on the completion of his doctoral work at the Ontario Institute for Studies in Education of the University of Toronto, Canada.

Jeanne M. Arnold is a fifth-grade teacher in Kenton, Ohio, USA. She received a B.S. and an M.A. from The Ohio State University. Her writing interests include research in the teaching of reading and writing, fiction for young readers, and humorous anecdotes for adults.

David Booth is a professor of education at the Ontario Institute for Studies in Education of the University of Toronto, Canada, where he teaches graduate courses in language development, the arts, children's literature, and literacy education. He has authored many teacher reference books and textbooks in all areas of language development—reading, writing, speaking and listening, drama and media—and has worked on several language arts curriculum guidelines for the Ontario Ministry of Education.

Cathy Bruce is an educator, writer, and researcher working with the Kawartha Pine Ridge District School Board in Peterborough, Ontario, Canada. She completed her master's work at the Ontario Institute for Studies in Education of the University of Toronto, Canada, and is currently a doctoral student in curriculum studies at the same university. Her interests are classroom-based research and effective teaching practices.

Sharon Lapkin is a professor in the Modern Language Centre and Second Language Education Program at the Ontario Institute for Studies in Education of the University of Toronto, Canada. She has published widely in the area of French second language education and is coeditor of the *Canadian Modern Language Review/La Revue canadienne des langues vivantes*.

Jennifer Lasenby is a doctoral candidate in the Department of Psychology at the University of Guelph in Ontario, Canada. She completed her master's thesis in the Human Development and Applied Psychology Department at the Ontario Institute for Studies in Education of the University of Toronto, Canada.

Carl Leggo is a poet and associate professor at the University of British Columbia, Vancouver, British Columbia, Canada, where he teaches undergraduate and graduate courses in writing and teaching. After 9 years of teaching in Newfoundland, he joined the Department of Language and Literacy Education, where he has been teaching, reading, researching, and writing for 13 years. He has published three books: *Growing Up Perpendicular on the Side of a Hill, View From My Mother's House,* and *Teaching to Wonder: Responding to Poetry in the Secondary Classroom.*

Jill Kedersha McClay is an associate professor in the Faculty of Education at the University of Alberta, Edmonton, Alberta, Canada, where she teaches graduate and undergraduate courses in language and literacy. Her research focus is composition theory and pedagogy, particularly the development of adolescents' writing in multimedia writing environments and teachers' practices in teaching composition.

Janette Pelletier is an assistant professor at the Institute of Child Study, Human Development and Applied Psychology at the Ontario Institute for Studies in Education of the University of Toronto, Canada. Her research projects include young children's beginning understandings of print, and metacognitive development and school readiness among first and second language learners.

Shelley Peterson teaches preservice and graduate literacy courses in the Department of Curriculum, Teaching and Learning at the Ontario Institute for Studies in Education of the University of Toronto, Canada. Her teaching and research interests are literacy instruction and assessment, with an emphasis on the sociocultural dimensions of classroom literacy learning and of classroom and large-scale writing assessment.

Donald S. Qi has taught English language subjects for school boards, colleges, and universities in Canada and China for many years. He has a doctorate in second language education from the Ontario Institute for Studies in Education of the University of Toronto, Canada. His dissertation examined the nature of language switching in the thinking processes that underlie second language task performance. He also has been a literacy assessor for the Toronto District School Board since 1993.

Monika Smith is a senior lecturer in German Studies at Victoria University of Wellington, New Zealand. She specializes in the teaching of German as a foreign language and in translation studies. She is currently enrolled in the doctoral program at the Ontario Institute for Studies in Education of the University of Toronto, Canada, where she researches collaborative approaches to L2 reading comprehension.

Pamela E. Van Nest teaches in the Early Literacy Program in Peterborough, Ontario, Canada, with the Kawartha Pine Ridge District School Board. She has been a special education teacher, consultant, and a primary classroom teacher in the state of Maine, USA, and in the province of Ontario, Canada, over the past 30 years.

Introduction

SHELLEY PETERSON

Teaching writing is truly a knotty endeavor. So much of what colleagues contributing to this book and I read about teaching writing is about how difficult it is. The title of Wood Ray and Laminack's (2001) recent book on teaching writing, for example, ends with *The Hard Parts (and They're All Hard Parts)*. Our own experiences as teachers of writers certainly underscore the authors' point. There are all sorts of little tangles in our daily teaching that are not so easily sorted out, in spite of our having read all the books about teaching writing that are available to us.

We find that much of the professional and academic literature on teaching writing addresses the interplay between process and product and the need to respect the contributions of individual writers' processes to the creations of their written products. Numerous colleagues—Nancie Atwell, Lucy McCormick-Calkins, Ralph Fletcher, Donald H. Graves, and Katie Wood Ray, among others—have contributed to our understanding of teaching writing by taking a look at the actual processes in which writers engage. These authors draw from the reflections of published writers (Murray, 1990) and from clinical studies of novice writers (Emig, 1971). Writing teachers, including me and other contributors to this book, have become much better managers of time and resources through reading this work. We also have gained a richer understanding of what is possible when writers have control over the various decisions involved in writing: choosing the topic and format, the audience, and the tone of their writing. There is no question that we have benefited enormously from the work of these writers and teachers of writing. Yet, like the teachers in *Writing Process Revisited: Sharing Our Stories* (Barnes, Morgan, & Weinhold, 1997), my fellow contributors and I find that what happens in our classrooms often falls short of the successes that are described in the resources that have so enriched our teaching. Issues such as those surrounding the diversity of language and cultures, or the use of various media and technologies, are left up to us as classroom teachers to work through as we interpret the theories and incorporate the practices in our own contexts. In this book, we take a closer look at some of the issues that began as tiny knots that we could ignore for a while but which eventually demanded our attention because they interfered with our students' learning and writing.

We use the knot metaphor to represent the difficult issues that sometimes become so entangled that they make us feel frustrated in our teaching. Our conversations about the knots of our teaching and writing evolved into this book. In each chapter, we tease out issues that are not often explicitly addressed in published teaching resources. We describe our attempts to untangle the difficult knots and our reflections on the untangling processes. These chapters represent our research, thinking, and practice as we begin to untangle those knots.

We have written this book for K–8 teachers who are interested in untangling some of the knots of writing instruction and assessment that persist in spite of all the good work that has been done in this field. We also expect this book to be useful in the teacher education courses in which these teachers are trained.

The book is organized in three sections. Section I, Students' and Teachers' Learning Processes, presents new twists on issues that have been significant to writing teachers since we were introduced to a process approach to teaching writing. Chapter 1 addresses the changes in teaching philosophy that are needed to adopt a process approach to teaching writing. Chapters 2 and 3 examine the contributions of oral language and interactions among writers to students' writing. Chapter 4 presents observations of beginning writers' development of theories about print.

Chapters 5 and 6 in section II, Diversity and Teaching Writing, address knots in teaching students whose primary language is not English. Chapter 7 examines the gender disparity in students' success as writers in classroom assessments and large-scale writing tests.

In section III, Teaching Writing Using Multimedia and the Arts, chapter 8 examines knots in the use of technology to connect writers from two different classes and grades, and chapter 9 addresses the fears that teachers and students have about teaching and learning poetry. Two chapters in this section explore ways to motivate reluctant writers and create challenging, meaningful classroom contexts for student writers: Chapter 10 advocates using drama, and chapter 11 proposes using popular culture in classrooms.

We represent people from various arenas of education—classroom and university teachers and school and school district administrators and consultants—who have come together to create this book from our passion and respect for writing and all that writing can contribute to our own and our students' lives. By bringing together the perspectives of teachers, administrators, consultants, and researchers on teaching writing, we hope to create new bridges between theory and practice.

REFERENCES

Barnes, D., Morgan, K., & Weinhold, K. (1997). *Writing process revisited: Sharing our stories*. Urbana, IL: National Council of Teachers of English.

Emig, J.A. (1971). *The composing process of twelfth graders* (Research Report No. 13). Urbana, IL: National Council of Teachers of English.

Murray, D. (1990). *Shoptalk: Learning to write with writers*. Portsmouth, NH: Heinemann.

Wood Ray, K., with Laminack, L.L. (2001). *The writing workshop: Working through the hard parts (and they're all hard parts)*. Urbana, IL: National Council of Teachers of English.

Students' and Teachers' Learning Processes

IN SECTION I, authors address issues that have been significant to writing teachers since the first writing instruction resources began appearing in teachers' professional libraries. The authors describe current research and reflect on their experiences as writing teachers, presenting a new twist on each issue.

This section begins with the story of a teacher who used a process approach to teaching writing for the first time after 27 years of teaching writing using a traditional approach. In chapter 1, Pamela E. Van Nest describes the knots she encountered and the ways that she untangled those knots as she began to use a process approach in her second-grade classroom.

Chapters 2 and 3 show how talk can help students untangle the knots of being unable to find ideas for their writing, of having difficulty developing ideas, and of being reluctant and/or finding it difficult to revise. In chapter 2, Jeanne M. Arnold and Shelley Peterson give examples of how particular teaching strategies and practices in a fifth-grade and an eighth-grade classroom encourage student interaction that supports students' writing. Jeanne describes two content area writing activities that are enhanced through students' talk while reading and writing newspaper articles and conducting role-play activities. Shelley identifies kinds of peer feedback that students find helpful in guiding revisions of their writing. In chapter 3, Cathy Bruce describes a strategy she used in bringing writers of different ages together to discuss their ideas and problems that arose as they wrote. She argues that multiage groups allow for productive and insightful discussion and problem solving for revisions.

Chapter 4 emphasizes the importance of using young children's theories about writing as a starting point for instruction. Janette Pelletier and Jennifer Lasenby examine these theories and present suggestions for teachers, arguing that merely providing opportunities to write may not be enough for many children: Teachers need to understand their students' theories about print in order to untangle knots in students' concepts of written language.

CHAPTER 1

Untangling Approaches to Teaching Writing: A Process of Change in One Classroom

PAMELA E. VAN NEST

The process of learning to become a writing teacher requires change and sorting through a tangle of practices that are not as effective as they can be in helping children become better writers. With that change come risks and challenges as well as satisfaction and accomplishment.

The opportunity to begin that change materialized while I was taking a graduate course titled *Teaching Writing*. As I began the course's required reading, I realized that I needed to untie the tangles of an old way of teaching (27 years' worth) and create a new tapestry that was more appropriate in my grade 2 classroom. My previous teaching experience had been concentrated around remedial reading and writing with children who had developmental disabilities. The writing process was often a painful, arduous task for the students and for me as the coach, cheerleader, and teacher. When I began teaching a "regular" class of children, I found that the methods for teaching writing I had used for 27 years no longer seemed appropriate.

Some of my old practices had been

- scheduling writing once or twice a week;
- giving all students the same story starter on which to build;
- requiring students to write in a daily journal, which I often used as busy work;
- revising and editing each child's work without his or her input;
- using predesigned worksheets to teach skills; and
- insisting that students work quietly by themselves.

I could see that the philosophy behind my long-tried practices centered on a view of the teacher as the controller of students' learning. Like Beaumier (1997),

> I told them what to write and when to write. I wanted to feel accountable for what the students were learning.... It was a combination of a number of things that helped me discover what was missing from my writing program. (pp. 87–88)

My old methods were fraying and unraveling as I began reading about researchers and educators (Calkins, 1994; Graves, 1994, 1996; Turbill, 1983) who advocated a student-centered philosophy supported by such practices as the following:

- students writing daily or at least three to four times a week for a sustained 15 to 30 minutes;
- students choosing their own writing topics;
- students beginning a new story each period, if desired, without finishing a previous piece;
- students helping one another with ideas, editing, and revising;
- students choosing writing buddies to share work; and
- using student writing to create minilessons for grammar, structure, or spelling.

These ideas and practical strategies were the very tools I needed to reshape the contrived and controlling way I had been teaching writing. Yet, I had many questions and anxieties about this writing workshop process. Graves (1994) and Calkins (1994) outline this process using slightly different terms, but it consists of essentially five steps: prewriting/rehearsal, writing, revising, editing, and publishing. Teachers can elaborate on any of the steps to help students in their own process.

First is the prewriting or rehearsal stage, in which students formulate the topic and ideas from that topic. In young children, this may take the form of a drawing, painting, clay sculpture, etc. In older students, story maps and other graphic organizers and peer conferencing give students a framework from which to work. I discovered that this process can look like idle sitting or twirling a pencil, which proved challenging to my concepts of being "on task."

Next is the actual writing, sometimes referred to as the draft or first copy. Students may generate multiple drafts and will be asked to read over their drafts and choose a piece that they would like to complete.

Step three is revising, an important part of which is rereading the piece selected for completion. A teacher conference with open-ended questions can sometimes spark new ideas, extensions, and deeper descriptions. Peers can help at this stage, but teachers must model positive techniques for students to use with one another to help a writer revise a piece of writing. This makes a classroom very busy and noisy with interactions happening in all parts of the room. This produced many anxieties and was quite a challenge to my old ideas about effective teaching.

Editing is usually the fourth step. Students scrutinize their work for corrections in punctuation, spelling, and usage. Again, modeling this process with students during minilessons will help them know what to look for to improve a piece of writing.

The final step is publishing. This can be as simple as the corrected "good copy" of a piece or as elaborate as producing a hard cover edition of a typed copy that is catalogued in the class library or in the school's library.

Could this process approach to teaching writing work for my students and me? The only way to discover why this process was so effective and how to implement it was to jump right in. And so I did.

My Journal of Change

When I began the process, I wondered what changes I would observe in my students' writing abilities and their attitudes about their writing. Equally important, I wondered if I could effectively change as a teacher. Could I unravel the entanglement of my former teaching habits to reflect a way of teaching writing that required me to share some control with my students? The following is a record of my personal reflections during this process of change in both my teaching methods and my attitude about students' abilities (all student names are pseudonyms).

January 25

My mind is flooded with fear, anxiety, "what ifs," images of utter chaos, of children running around with no writing being done, and foreboding thoughts of being scrutinized by my principal this week. Crazy daydreams of me bumbling through explanations of this new venture in the midst of criticisms from colleagues and parents hover in my mind as I gather the students and introduce a new process of learning to write. What will really happen when I let the students write anything they want and announce that we will write EVERY DAY? Nagging doubts arise in my head, clattering, chanting, raising all the bits of inadequacy I feel deep in my soul. My first defense is usually one of immediate shutdown. I feel that I can't do this—it's too hard and I won't try. But I have to try. This writing process is current and fresh learning for me—a real challenge to my past methods that did not encourage a higher level thinking approach for students. I realize that the old teacher-directed ways will not develop students' potential in writing. I push the anxieties and doubts aside and begin.

I gather the class together to tell them about our new routine. I explain that I, too, go to school to learn about teaching writing. The group becomes very quiet, the kind of quiet that tells me that students are curious, interested, focused. I explain that each of them will have a "writing buddy" who will listen to the stories they write. Each person will work with this buddy for a month. I want to avoid the "popularity" contest that happens when students choose their partners, so I choose the partners. I hear a few moans but many sounds of delight. The children receive yellow practice books that are to be their "Writing Ideas" books.

Some students wonder if they can take the notebooks home, and others want to know if they can write a story right now. This positive reaction from students gives me a glimpse of hope, of success for them as well as for me. A sense of relief floods over me. The doubt and anxious feelings stop short and fade. Where will all of this lead? My new tapestry of teaching writing begins.

Although I have no previous experience with this process, I have a feeling that I will see certain results. I predict that my average to below-average readers will struggle with this method of writing with so much expected independence, and my above-average readers will have no problem with this process and become very fluent in their writing.

(As it turned out, my predictions were not entirely correct. I found many reluctant readers and writers writing more stories and improving the organization of their stories. My fluent readers had no difficulty writing beyond the first few ideas on paper, except for one student who could not [or would not] write more than two or three sentences about a topic.)

January 26

Last week during my graduate course, the professor presented an activity to get our ideas flowing for an upcoming assignment. We listed categories and ideas as suggested from the resource text BECOMING BETTER WRITERS (Peterson, 1995). These suggestions ignited a topic for me and inspired two hours of writing the next evening in preparation for the first assignment—writing a narrative. Perhaps these very categories will do the same for my students.

I explain to the students how to use the first few pages of our writing book as a place to gather ideas. The students draw a line down the middle of the page and write the word CATEGORY on one side and IDEAS on the other. I explain first what the word CATEGORY means. We start with the suggestion of "sports" as a category. This draws in the boys. In my experience, boys seem to be more reluctant than girls in writing so I want to appeal to their interests in the hope that they can become more interested in writing. Five or six youngsters contribute their ideas. As one student shares, another hand goes up. I am encouraged. One of the girls shares her category, "pets." This inspires more suggestions from others. I demonstrate how to write the next category halfway down the page on the left, using the right-hand column for ideas and words about that sport or pet. The next direction to the class is to begin writing for 20 minutes using the ideas written in their notebooks.

Some students' faces change from calm to serious concern, others from calm to frustration. The first request is "How do you spell...?" My past practice had been to write the correct spelling on the board. I acted like an automated spelling machine, often eliciting the spelling from the students by sounding out the word. This time I ask students to try it on their own because I do not want to discourage the free flowing of ideas. Graves (1994) and Calkins (1994) write about not getting bogged down in correct spelling, allowing time to keep the ideas flowing. Stopping to spell a word "perfectly" stilts the process of writing. By encouraging students not to worry about the exact spelling right now, I have loosened a well-used square knot in my old approach to teaching writing!

I walk around the room and encourage students, asking them what they know about the categories they have chosen. Eric's frustration erupts in whining. Because he is an emergent reader, I help him one on one to focus his ideas by letting him dictate them to me. He does no writing on this day, but instead draws pictures of some ideas for his story. I am encouraged to accept his drawings as a writing effort by Calkins (1994), who says that drawing is a very important element of emergent writing.

After 20 minutes, the students join their writing buddies in a whole-group lesson. I tell them that they will read what they have written to their buddies and then their buddies will talk about their writing. I model for students how to ask one another about parts of their story or the characters. I use prompts such as "I'd like to know more about...," "I wonder what that character looks like?" "What colour is the...?" "I really like the...in your story" or "I hope you tell us more about...." I explain that this can help their buddies with more ideas for their stories. The room hums with activity as the pairs are focused on their task.

January 27

Students write for about half an hour. During this time I have a conference with four students. Graves (1994), Calkins (1994), and Peterson (1995) explain that these meetings can be very brief. They are opportunities to check in with the writer and to offer encouragement, as well as to assess areas of strength and weakness. In this conference the students read their story to me. I use the phrase, "I wonder what..." when asking one child about an aspect of her story and other phrases, such as "I really like the way you use the word...," to give feedback to other children. I tell students what I can "see" in my mind or that I wonder what color, size, smell, etc. a particular object or character is in the story. I base my questions on Power's (1997) recommendations. I notice that students' stories are longer than those written in September. Students are staying on topic, as well.

Eric continues to be frustrated during the writing period. He is a very reluctant writer who finds writing really difficult. I again try writing key ideas with him, this time about his favorite subject of hockey. I use the "dictate and copy" strategy that I had used in special education classes for years. Jerome is also a challenge because he sits staring off into space instead of writing. I suggest that we try a story map and show him how one idea connects to another. This does not inspire him. He continues to find other things in his desk to look at. I remind myself that writing is a thinking process. Ideas sometimes need to float about the mind before they find their way to paper. Yet, avoiding a task at hand can look very similar. I feel frustration rising, but move on to assist other children.

February 3

I feel I'm not in control during the reading and writing period. When students work with buddies to edit spelling, their attention fluctuates and the relative quiet working environment breaks down. I again find myself feeling frustration and tension. I wonder what would happen if the principal walked in and perceived this working period as chaotic. My new experience in grade 2 is being overshadowed by years and years of expectations of having quiet, focused students. My "Anxiety Committee" has been meeting again in my head, critically shrieking to me, "A noisy classroom is unproductive and run by an incompetent teacher!"

There, that's better now. The noise level is kept to a working hush. These changing perceptions of teaching writing are forcing me also to change my perceptions of a "good teacher" and of "good" classroom management. I realize I have deeper issues to look at and that they have nothing to do with the way students write.

February 6

Besides teaching writing I also must address the curriculum demands of social studies. I decide to combine the two. I assign a writing piece that will be about "Places in Canada." This breaks away from my new practice of giving students free choice of topics. Each student must write about a place they have visited in Canada. I use guiding questions such as, "What does it look like in this place?" and "What did you see or hear while you were there?"

Only one student appears to be inspired and writes as he has never done before. He records his experiences visiting Manitoulin Island, Ontario. Five pages and counting! The other students are not writing much at all. Perhaps the assigned topic did not fit their ideas and this requirement with a deadline is blocking their writing. This demonstrates to me the creative power of the process approach.

February 21

We had a whole-class "author group" yesterday. All the students read their writing. The group at large then posed questions and comments to the author. It was an opportunity to model phrases such as "I really like the word ___ you used" or "I like the part...." The students need more practice with this type of positive feedback. I realize how mistake-oriented my students are at this early age. We practice commenting on the positive first before finding errors. This is a lesson that I, too, must remember.

February 26

The other grade 2 class in the school also has been using the writing process approach. Students recently published their stories. My colleague edits and types each story. The students then make a cover, laminate it, and submit it to the school library for cataloguing and attach a borrower's sign-out card. These works become a permanent part of the school library and are shelved along with other authors' works. Some of my students ask if they can submit their stories to the library. This gives students authentic authorship and an authentic purpose for writing. With some parental help, I think we can accomplish this.

February 28

Graves (1996) claims that if teachers themselves write and share their work with students, the children will see real writing modeled. Today I am trying this element in the writing process. I write at a desk alongside my students for the first seven minutes before I get up and conference with them. I explain to students that I also want to write a story during this time, so I need time to write without being disturbed. As I sit and write, I feel an urge to get up and see how everyone is doing. It feels very awkward sitting at a desk "doing my own thing." One very soothing result of my initiative this morning is the quiet.

I realize that I am experiencing the "what-to-write" dilemma. Sitting and thinking are important parts of writing! Once again I realize that the real change in this whole endeavor is the change in my teaching behavior. When in 27 years have I ever taken 10 minutes to write something meaningful during a writing period? NEVER. This new tapestry is really taking shape.

March 1

During writing time, I am revising my draft of a story inspired from a book that I read to students. I am playing with a narrative approach that leads me to a form of poetry. Instead of full sentences, my writing changes to short phrases about feelings and impressions this book is evoking in me. I feel frustrated that I can no longer sit and continue this piece. I need more time to develop it. But it is time to circulate and conference with students. How often have students felt that same frustration in wanting to continue with a flow of ideas as I announce that it is time to change activities?

March 8

We try another technique in the writing process approach, peer conferencing. This is a new stitch pattern for my teaching style. Students sit with their writing buddy and listen to each other's writing. This is just as important as a teacher-student conference, according to Graves (1994). I'm willing to give it a try. In the past few weeks, students have chosen their own writing buddies and I have modeled author groups with the whole class. I read to them a short piece I have written for my course. Students give me ideas how to improve my story. Today we try a group of four students listening to one another. I move around the room listening and guiding their questions. I listen to one group as they share this process, yet I am distracted by the noise of the group in the far corner. As one girl, Tanya, finishes reading her piece, the two boys in her group ask about various aspects of her subject and suggest some ideas. Tanya jots down the suggestions! [Later she actually incorporates them into her writing!] This is a moment that gives me encouragement to continue. I am in awe of how grade 2 students can respond to one another in this inspiring way.

March 9

Today we are writing a thank-you note to a student's aunt for supplying us with carpet squares. I am scribing for the class as we brainstorm what to say and how to say it. This is the composing modeling that Graves (1994) wrote about. I am writing whatever the students suggest. We then reread it each time. During this procedure we decide if there are any changes that need to be made. We decide which sentences are repeats and which sentences need to be put together—real editing on a joint project. Although it looks messy with lines and arrows, it models how we have "permission" to make mistakes and to change our thoughts as we write. It is one of those truly authentic teaching moments where the lesson has a real use and therefore real meaning.

March 19

Although I am closely following the designs of those who have gone before me, I know that this process with this class and with others to come, like exquisite knotted lace, will take on a life of its own. We, students and teacher, will design a more effective and successful routine in this writing process as we move from brainstorming to book making. As I continue practicing and expanding the strategy of writing with children during writing time, sharing that writing, conferencing with students daily (if possible), scheduling peer conferences and author groups, and developing student-centered minilessons, my confidence and skill level will improve. Already it seems natural to talk about a student's piece of writing by saying, "I really like how..." and "I wonder what...looks like." This is a powerful and positive change from my past practices.

Thinking About the Changes

After years of remedial teaching in which I used a structured approach to teaching writing and always used story starters, I can see now that the process approach with which I have experimented is more enriching for students. I cannot turn back to those older, more controlling methods. The directions are not so unfamiliar now, the pattern no longer a jumble of kinks and twists needing patient straightening out. This experience has shed light on many positive aspects of the writing process and on my awareness of students' abilities. I have learned that a process approach helps grade 2 students find their writing "voices," that distinctive personality of writing in which I can actually "hear" the writers through their writing. I am sure that writing almost every day is important, even though I started this practice late in the school year. I believe that sometimes the process of writing takes place in the moment while just sitting or twirling a pencil as the writer rereads previous works. Often, this is when new ideas begin to grow.

I once heard a woman say, "Most of the time we don't realize what a satisfying and exciting process learning is until we become proactive and engage with it fully." This experiment in challenging and changing my teaching techniques has been both exciting and overwhelming. It encourages me to take risks again, reworking the stubborn twists into a beautiful tapestry that will enrich my teaching and my students' learning.

REFERENCES

Beaumier, T. (1997). Beyond reading and writing: Realizing each child's potential. In D. Barnes, K. Morgan, & K. Weinhold (Eds.), *Writing process revisited: Sharing our stories* (pp. 81–97). Urbana, IL: National Council of Teachers of English.

Calkins, L.M. (1994). *The art of teaching writing* (2nd ed.). Portsmouth, NH: Heinemann.

Graves, D.H. (1989). *Writing: Teachers and children at work*. Portsmouth, NH: Heinemann.

Graves, D.H. (1994). *A fresh look at writing*. Portsmouth, NH: Heinemann.

Graves, D.H. (1996). Teaching writing. If you write, they will too. *Instructor, 105*(5), 40–41.

Peterson, S. (1995). *Becoming better writers*. Edmonton, AB: Hendriks.

Power, B. (1997). Teaching writing: Ask better questions—Get better writers. *Instructor, 107*(4), 60–61.

Turbill, J. (1983). *No better way to teach writing!* Portsmouth, NH: Heinemann.

CHAPTER 2

Untangling Knots Through Talking About Writing

JEANNE M. ARNOLD AND SHELLEY PETERSON

In this chapter, we write about students we have worked with, discussing our thoughts and observations on how to make the most of talk in writing classrooms. We apply the work of researchers who value talk as a tool for exploring and clarifying ideas before, during, and after students write (Barnes, 1992; Britton, 1970; Freedman, 1992). These researchers explain that students introduce one another to a broader base of ideas, knowledge, and perspectives than would be possible if they wrote in isolation.

Our suggestions show how talk can help students untangle the knots of being stuck for ideas for their writing and having difficulty in developing ideas and characters. Whereas Cathy Bruce and Joseph Allin (see chapter 3 and chapter 8) discuss the ways in which Internet interactions and multiage author groups help to untangle these knots, we write about talk among same-age students within a grade 5 and a grade 8 classroom.

Jeanne's Thoughts and Observations

When I first began to teach, I took the view that children learn to write by writing multiple drafts, examining and improving the writing with each draft. But, what I have begun to learn is that when children write in a vacuum of their own thoughts, their ideas do not seem to become more sophisticated and diverse. Often, they repeat the same mistakes.

I looked for a way to untie the knots of "treadmill thinking," in which my fifth-grade students repeated the same tired ideas and overworked words and showed a lack of new perspectives. At first, I tried conferencing with each student about his or her writing, offering suggestions and new ways to approach writing. This helped some students, but there were two large, looming drawbacks—one was the time involved in trying to meet with each student for a meaningful discussion, and the second was that students seemed to write verbatim whatever I told them in their conferences. I was not looking for a parroting of my suggestions; I wanted students to take ideas we talked about in conferences and develop them on their own.

As the specter of my American state's proficiency tests clouded the horizon, I grew concerned that my students would not demonstrate how bright and capable they are through their writing. I worried that they might not be able to write clearly enough or include enough details to be given full credit for their answers. This would hurt them not only in the writing portion of the proficiency test but also in each of the other areas in which extended responses are required. As my students practiced for the proficiency tests, I made an observation that changed the way I teach writing: Open discussion with peers made a great deal of difference in the quality of students' writing.

Peer Conversations About Students' Writing

During the week, students practiced writing summaries, personal narratives, various letters, persuasive pieces, and responses to social studies and science questions. As this work progressed, I encouraged students to discuss their ideas with others, editing their work as they went. The difference between the rough drafts and the final products was truly amazing. Once the students had a chance to talk with their peers about their ideas and stories, the final products were filled with more ideas, better word choices, and even better spelling attempts.

First, students gave feedback on one another's work through comments such as "That beginning is boring" or "This first sentence doesn't really make me want to read your story." Students did not offer specific suggestions but rather opinions of the value of the piece of writing. Second, and perhaps more important, students began to develop their own ideas by bouncing them off others. I began to hear comments such as "That's a good story, but what if she had something weird about her," or "That would be funnier if the germ could actually talk or if we treated him like a wanted killer." Those comments helped the writers to develop their stories in novel and interesting ways.

I was surprised that the discussion actually led to each story being very different, rather than leading to stories that all sounded alike. Each story showed the writer's own thoughts.

One day, I did something different that led to my discovery of the importance of talk in students' writing. I asked students to write a personal narrative or other short story in an environment similar to that of the state proficiency test. I separated students' desks and did not allow discussion. Even though I gave the students more time to develop their own ideas and encouraged them to use various graphic aids to lay out their ideas, these pieces of writing did not come close to the quality of their weekly practice writing. What was the difference? How were these students able to write such interesting, detailed pieces during their weekly practice sessions but not able to do so in the proficiency test settings? The biggest factor seemed to be the discussions, which allowed these students to try out their ideas for different audiences and helped them clarify their knowledge and ideas about certain subjects.

Research supports my observations. Wells and Chang-Wells (1992) emphasize the importance to students' learning of opportunities for taking part in meaningful context-embedded interactions. Without being engaged in conversation with others, children have little opportunity to explore ideas, clarify them, and make them their own. Furthermore, children do not learn how to express their own ideas or how to make their voices heard in ways that give them control over their lives. Lindfors (1987) furthers this idea by stating, "Interaction, it appears, can help one go beyond his own limits by providing a new idea, question or observation; by providing cognitive conflict; and by providing collaborative assistance" (p. 274). In addition, talk enables children to achieve a number of purposes (Halliday, 1969): to satisfy needs, to control others' behavior, to get along with others, to express individuality, to seek and test knowledge, to imagine new worlds, and to communicate information. Children who learn the power of language to achieve these purposes in conversation have a strong foundation for using writing as a tool to serve a wide range of functions in their everyday lives.

Classroom Conversations Leading to Writing

Now a strong advocate of conversation to support students' writing, I help students develop ideas for their content area writing through end-of-class discussions. For example, at the end of a science period, my students discuss what they have learned, how it will affect their lives, and what this subject matter means to the world at large.

When I began the discussion periods by asking open-ended questions, there were the inevitable moments in which everyone stared at one another and said nothing. I found that many of my students had not had the experience of verbally organizing their thoughts. They felt that they could not give an opinion because they had rarely been asked to express one. Initially, the discussions involved me talking about my views on a particular piece of fiction, a current event, or something personal. Within a few days, I invited students into the discussions. When someone ventured an opinion, I always praised and validated the opinion to encourage others to participate. From these discussions, I asked students to write about their discoveries. The following, written by four students in my class, came from these discussions and was sent to the mayor and city council:

> Many kids in Kenton like to skateboard or roller blade. It is a very popular sport. The problem for us is that there are no safe places to do this activity. Some kids have been hurt by riding on sidewalks and city streets, or have gotten in trouble with the police. It is also unsafe to skate in the parking lots of the shopping centers because of cars and pedestrians. We are asking the city council to consider finding some land in a park or other area that could be used to build a skate park. Maybe someone would be willing to donate a little land for us to use. It wouldn't need to be really big. In return, we would be willing to have some fund-raisers to help pay for the building of ramps and other stuff we would need. Thank you for hearing our request and helping to keep kids safe.

I also found success using the local newspaper as a starting point for discussion that led to writing. I tore out sections of the paper that were within the understanding and interest areas of fifth-grade children, divided the students into groups, gave them an article to read and analyze, and then opened the room for discussions. I asked students to paraphrase the article so others who had not read it would be able to understand the subject matter. Early in the year, students had difficulty with this activity because they were unfamiliar with the layout of newspapers and with some of the vocabulary. After a few weeks, however, students learned how to read a newspaper and were keen to see the next week's issue. A student wrote the following in response to a news report about a convicted murderer walking into a school and stealing some items while school was in session:

> We just read a newspaper article about a man coming into a school and stealing stuff. Can you believe this?! People are coming into schools and stealing during school hours. Some of them are wanted killers! I think someone could come in and claim they were a kids parent and take them and kill them. I think there should be a security system or at least a sign-in sheet for every school that everybody who comes in must sign. That way no one would get hurt. In Lima a killer was coming in during school hours and stealing whatever he pleased. Someone could have been killed! I am worried sometimes. Lima isn't very far away from us.

At the end of the year, I asked students to write a class newspaper. They were wildly excited about practicing some of the techniques they had learned about writing informational news items, persuasive editorials and advertisements, and narratives of interesting events. My students were particularly avid "Letter to the Editor" writers. They were fascinated by the idea of being able to express an opinion that could be published in their local newspaper. They also wrote letters to their principal and school superintendent about issues relevant to students' lives:

> Central Elementary fifth graders get only one very short recess out of a $6\frac{1}{2}$ hour day. This makes kids tired from sitting in a chair a little more than 6 hours. When we get tired it makes it hard to pay attention. This leads to us not learning the lesson for the day. This could affect our whole future. Because of this, we might never get a good job to support our family. That might lead to our kids having a bad childhood. I think we could solve this by having at least another morning or afternoon recess. I hope you consider my request and save a kid's future.

> My complaint is the school food. I think it tastes bad. Who cares if it is "fat free" or "nutritious." For example, the macaroni tastes like rubber, and they now are making the bread sticks in greasy butter. If we want butter, we should put it on ourselves...we're big kids, its not like our mommies have to do it! I know what you are going to respond to this "Why don't they just pack!" Well, some kids don't have time to do it or nothing good to eat. So, now to my point; we should get something like the middle school where you pick out your food from a bigger selection, or machines. Thank you for considering my suggestion.

I used role-play to help students develop their oral and written communication skills, as well (for further reading about the contributions of role-play to students' writing, see chapter 10). When studying the U.S. Civil War, I asked students to prepare, produce, and perform a reenactment of nine scenes from this time period. In completing this assignment, students researched, wrote, and performed historically accurate scenes, in addition to designing costumes and sets. Students enjoyed learning the syntax and vocabulary that were particular to this historical period, creating scripts that used period language. The following welcome speech was written jointly by two students for the opening of their reenactment. The piece that follows the welcome depicts President and Mrs. Lincoln having a dinner party the night before he signs the Emancipation Proclamation, abolishing slavery in the United States:

I imagine y'all are Yankee School Children come here to learn more about the Civil War. I should introduce myself. I am Mrs. Jefferson Davis. My husband was quite famous during the time of the Civil War. You see, the states didn't always get along as well as they do now. In the early 1860s the states in the North began fighting with the states in the South. They were fighting because the Northern states didn't approve of the Southern states keeping slaves. So in 1861, seven southern states decided to leave the Union and form their own country. My husband, Jefferson Davis, was elected the President of these Southern states. Abraham Lincoln was elected the President of the Northern States. Neither side could agree on what to do about the problem of slavery, so a long war began, lasting until 1865. For 4 long years, people fought and died in battles to keep things the way they wanted them to be. Eventually all the states made up and came back together to form the United States of America, where we live together in peace. The scenes you will see today will show you how life was during this time in our American history known as the Civil War.

Mr. Lincoln:	Well, tomorrow will be a historical day I hope. I've decided to go ahead and sign the Emancipation Proclamation.
Guest 1 (male):	Why will it be important?
Mr. Lincoln:	It will free the slaves in the whole country and it will keep new states from allowing slavery when they are formed.
Guest 2 (male):	Don't you think it will cause the war to go on and on since the South will never agree to let their slaves go?
Mrs. Lincoln:	Abe, aren't you afraid of what will happen if you sign this?
Mr. Lincoln:	I think it may cause the war to go on longer, but in the end the south will see that we are right in this. Yes, I am afraid of what will happen, but am more afraid of how our country will be in the future if I don't sign it. We must make peace and work together to become a strong country.
Guest 3 (female):	This may make someone want to kill you. Some people will not forgive you for doing this.
Mr. Lincoln:	I am more sure of this than anything I have ever done. Death may happen, but this is right. I will sign it tomorrow. Are you all with me?
All:	Yes, we will support you! (They stand and raise their glasses in a toast.)

I observed that the students' talk about the U.S. Civil War greatly enriched their writing. They showed a depth of understanding about the conflicts and issues of the war. They also demonstrated a level of empathy for the decision makers and for the people whose lives were so greatly affected by the Civil War that would not have been possible if the students had been asked to write independently without ongoing discussion.

Shelley's Thoughts and Observations

My examples of how oral language contributes to students' writing are drawn from a case study research project in an eighth-grade classroom. Like Jeanne, the eighth-grade classroom teacher, Andrew (all names from the research study are pseudonyms), was looking for ways to help students develop their ideas and use more description and details in their writing. To begin untangling the knot, Andrew used literature as a starting point for discussion that led to writing. His goal was to foster eighth graders' talk about character development in published literature as a starting point for developing characters for their own narratives. They began by reading a description of Cal, the father of protagonist Burl, in *The Maestro* (Wynne-Jones, 1995):

> It was odd for Burl to hear his father whistle. Cal was quiet most often, a sullen kind of quiet like thunder a long way off. Then all of a sudden he could Texas two-step himself into a rage and send things hurtling across the room: a plate of mashed potatoes, a broken shoe, a chair with you in it—whatever came to hand. You had to hold onto your seat when Cal was like that.
>
> The whistling led Burl to believe that his father was not in one of those thunderhead moods. It gave him the nerve to go on.
>
> It was a foolish game, trailing a man like Cal. But Burl still recalled a time when his father took him places, showed him things....
>
> Cal had taken to rubbing Burl's nose in things. "Whose limp minnow is this anyway, Dolly?" Burl's mother, Doloris, knew better than to answer. (p. 7)

Andrew asked students to talk in small groups about Cal's personality. They came up with words such as *mean, violent,* and *unpredictable* to describe Cal. Then students talked about the ways in which Wynne-Jones shows readers that Cal was mean, violent, and unpredictable. Students identified the descriptions of Cal's actions, the things he said, and Burl's memories of his father as strategies used by the author. Andrew asked students to try out similar strategies to develop characters for their narratives. He encouraged students to talk about their writing with peers in groups of four or five students as they wrote.

Following is a small part of a conversation between students Jake and David, who adopted the strategy used by Wynne-Jones in describing characters through their actions. Similar to conversations among many students in their eighth-grade class, the boys' conversation provided a forum for writers to play with ideas that they were considering for their writing.

Jake:	David, I got another idea. Do you think I should say it was the day before he was about to climb Everest, and it was a dream? So, like, saying something like a really terrifying moment in his dream?
David:	Yeah.
Jake:	And then his climb happening or not.
David:	You have to be careful that you don't confuse readers.
Jake:	Because I wrote, "As I got to the top of Everest, I screamed, 'I'm on top of the world.' Before I knew it, I was noticing the ice, snow and rock under me cracking. I thought to myself, 'Oh no, this could be bad.' As all this rock, snow, and ice was pounding me in the head, I thought about everything. It was like my whole life was passing before me."
David:	Maybe you could say, "I saw myself at the age of 3...."
Jake:	No, I've already written out his whole life, well the first 20 years of it.
David:	First 20 years?
Jake:	I only did, like, two or three paragraphs for, like, every other year—his second birthday, he joined a hockey team.
David:	There's hockey?
Jake:	No, it's not...
David:	You know what you might want to do? Everything in his life that made him want to climb Mount Everest and all that. Like what gave him the strength.
Jake:	He likes the cold because he likes snowmobiling and all that. I don't know.

Jake eventually cut the entire section he had written on the sequence of events leading up to the protagonist's Mount Everest climb because he felt it did not contribute to the development of his character. His conversation with David provided an opportunity to play with the idea of developing his character through the flashback, working out particular possibilities and problems in using this technique, even though he decided not to use the flashback in his final piece of writing. This type of problem solving would not have been available to Jake if he had been told to write quietly at his desk.

Peer talk also provided information about the audience's responses to students' writing. In another conversation in which David voiced an unfavorable emotional response to the protagonist's cannibalistic activities, Jake came to see that his audience might not appreciate the graphic descriptions he had written. His final draft softened the details of the cannibalization. Similarly, when peers read each other's writing and responded with questions about the plausibility of the content or with a request for more information to help them better understand the writing, students revised their writing to address the questions.

I observed that informal conversation among students while they wrote influenced the number and quality of revisions that students were willing to make, as well. Jake wrote seven drafts over a 13-week period and the other three case study students wrote from three to five drafts. Unlike students in other studies of students' revisions to their writing (Bridwell, 1980; Faigley & Witte, 1981), Andrew's eighth graders made more higher level revisions (adding, deleting, or moving words, phrases, and sentences) than lower level edits. Andrew's eighth graders, unlike students in the aforementioned studies, were given ample time to write and to talk with peers and their teacher as they wrote.

Final Thoughts and Cautions

Through our classroom teaching and research, we find that opportunities for students to "speak authentically of what they know and imagine" (Peterson, 1992, p. 51) while they write is essential to furthering students' writing development and their learning across the curriculum. Talk that allows students to play with ideas for their writing, that asks for clarification about confusing details, that shows readers' emotional responses to the writing, or that questions the believability of the writing provides writers with useful information for creating and developing ideas in their writing. Students' positive responses to their peers' writing help to create a sense of belonging within the classroom social network, as well. Talk while writing helps students to untangle knots in finding ideas for their writing and in developing a sense of the topics, characters, and events that their peer audience will enjoy reading and respond favorably to.

However, by providing opportunities for students to respond to each other's writing, teachers may inadvertently set a new tangle in motion. Students who receive feedback that embarrasses them by pointing out failings in the writing or that ridicules their choice of topics, characters, events, or language will link writing endeavors with hurtful social experiences. Our observations show that students' fear of embarrassment through peers' responses to their writing may create a new knot of reluctance to write.

We find that it is important for teachers to model and reinforce positive social and communication skills to ensure that students treat one another with respect when they provide verbal feedback to their peers. In Jeanne's fifth-grade class and in Andrew's eighth-grade class, the teachers monitor how well students show empathy toward their peers when discussing each other's writing. They also ask students to talk about the kinds of feedback that they find useful in their writing and model these kinds of feedback in their own interactions with their students. They recognize that the contributions that talk can make to students' writing can be diminished if students use the talk to embarrass their peers. Although the teachers value classrooms that hum with children's talk, they realize that the knots of student apprehension about finding and developing ideas will untangle only when students feel secure that they and their writing will be valued and respected by everyone in the class.

REFERENCES

Barnes, D. (1992). *From communication to curriculum*. Portsmouth, NH: Boynton/Cook.

Bridwell, L.S. (1980). Revising strategies in twelfth grade students' transactional writing. *Research in the Teaching of English, 14*(3), 197–222.

Britton, J. (1970). *Language and learning*. New York: Penguin.

Faigley, L., & Witte, S. (1981). Analyzing revision. *College Composition and Communication, 32*(4), 400–414.

Freedman, S.W. (1992). Outside-in and inside-out: Peer response groups in two ninth-grade classes. *Research in the Teaching of English, 26*(1), 71–107.

Halliday, M.A.K. (1969). Relevant models of language. *Educational Review, 22*(1), 26–37.

Lindfors, J.W. (1987). *Children's language and learning* (2nd ed.). Englewood Cliffs, NJ: Prentice Hall.

Peterson, R. (1992). *Life in a crowded place: Making a learning community*. Portsmouth, NH: Heinemann.

Wells, G., & Chang-Wells, G.L. (1992). *Constructing knowledge together: Classrooms as centers of inquiry and literacy*. Portsmouth, NH: Heinemann.

LITERATURE CITED

Wynne-Jones, T. (1995). *The maestro*. Toronto: Douglas & McIntyre.

CHAPTER 3

Multiage Author Groups: One Way to Untangle the Revision Knot

CATHY BRUCE

As a writer and a teacher of student writers, I have been bothered persistently by the inadequacies of my own revision strategies and those that I have used with students. I often have thought to myself that there must be a secret and wonderful way out there to revise writing that is eluding me and is just beyond my grasp. The search for more interesting, helpful, and motivating ways to revise writing has led me back to the same conclusion: Revising writing—no matter how you do it—is hard work. Reordering, adding detail, changing words to improve description, writing a different transition, and connecting the ending to the beginning are some of the elements of the revision process that many writers would like to eliminate altogether in our impatience to arrive at a stellar, polished text. At the same time, we also know that the care taken with the revisions is a critical step in creating a rich piece of writing.

This particular knot—the twistings and turnings, the likes and dislikes of the revising process—becomes even more entangled when we deal with students in the classroom. So often, students have come to me with a first draft in hand stating, "I'm done!" with a clear message that revising was not on their agenda.

Writing and revising in the classroom setting often involves peer discussion. Talking, listening, and writing are a natural triad in communication and, indeed, are cornerstones for making meaning in our world for ourselves and for others (Bruner, 1991; Wells, 1999; Wertsch & Toma, 1995). In classrooms, writing conferences emphasize talking and listening about writing in a one-to-one setting. Atwell (1998) describes how to frame one-to-one writing conferences by beginning with the writer explaining what he or she wants from the conference and then having the "responder" listen and respond in ways that will help the writer. A further extension of pairs conferencing is the use of author groups (Graves, 1989) in which writers meet as a group and offer suggestions and observations about one another's writing. All group members are writers seeking feedback. This is different from the feedback received from the teacher during traditional teacher-student writing conferences, in which the student acts as writer and the teacher acts as editor, and it is certainly different from written comments on a paper. The group members are all writers and all responders. In this sense, the playing field is leveled.

Participating in author groups has helped me as a writer work through text with the support of fellow writers. More important, it has improved my interest in and enthusiasm for revising my own writing. After meeting with other writers, I am more eager to get back to the text for revisions. Whereas when I work in isolation, I dread going back to revise my own writing. In the latter case, it is as though I am the writer, the audience, and the critic all at once. Worse yet, my deadlines are self-imposed and easier to break.

Generally, author groups have writers that are approximately the same age. I believe that this is primarily because of the structure of schools in which children are most often grouped by same age and grade in classrooms, making it most convenient for these students to work together. Same-age and same-grade author groups are also a way for teachers to foster a positive, safe, and supportive classroom community because the students take risks together as writers.

On the other hand, I have observed some of the limitations of writers working with same-age peers. My own experience with same-age writers is that the group members are very sympathetic to the ideas presented in writing because the members have had similar experiences. The ease and flow of the group discussion and comments in author groups begins to make me wonder whether individuals' being similar in age and life experience makes them less critical of one another. Do they make leaps of faith because the themes in the texts of other writers in the group are so close to their own experiences? Is there a lack of richness in the perspectives brought to the writing group because of the homogeneous demographic nature of the members? Are the members too much the same? Multiage author groups may address some of these questions.

Multiage Author Groups

Limited documentation of multiage author groups exists, and so I wanted to try them myself with some willing writers. I wanted to know more about how an author group functions when the members of the group represent a wide range of ages.

I turned to a familiar source in order to conduct and document a multiage author group. My sister's family took a year to travel around the world. The children (one girl and one boy) were being home schooled for the year and would return to the public school system for the beginning of the next school year. I proposed to the family that the daughter (Sarah, age 13), the son (Connor, age 10), and the mother (Connie, age 40), along with myself (age 35), form an author group for a period of time when we were visiting and traveling together.

We participated in the prewriting, drafting, and revising stages of writing together over the course of six days. Each member of the group was a different age and at a different stage of comfort with writing. Sarah enjoyed writing and maintained a journal during the family travels. She was an avid reader, as well. Connor was a reluctant writer who infrequently read short novels independently. He was an excellent sculptor of miniature characters using soft clay-like materials. I loved to write but found the revision stage very challenging. My sister, Connie, had not written narrative text in years, although during the family travels she wrote letters home to share the adventures with friends and family.

This is the story of one family group of writers. It is my hope that some parts of the story will resonate with the reader and initiate some new thoughts about how elementary classroom writing programs can be structured to support student writers. My example is an entry point to further studies of multiage author groups and perhaps an opening of a door to thinking about multiage author groups in schools. As Stake (1995) emphasizes, "The real business of case study is particularization, not generalization. We take a particular case and come to know it well, not primarily as to how it is different from others but what it is, what it does" (p. 8). I will discuss the ways in which what I have learned from this case study might be adapted to the elementary classroom setting.

To begin the process with the author group, I proposed an agenda to the group that highlighted what we could do for approximately one hour each day over the course of six days (see Figure 3.1).

The hour we spent writing each day might be similar to a classroom schedule during which students would be involved in a language program for about an hour each day. Members of the group agreed that this was a reasonable agenda to follow, although Connor was concerned that one hour of author group activities each day would be a very significant

FIGURE 3.1
CHRONOLOGY OF WRITING-RELATED ACTIVITY

Day One
- brainstorm ideas as individuals
- brainstorm as a group
- begin writing

Day Two
- personal writing
- group update (this is what I'm doing, where I might go)

Day Three
- personal writing
- sharing first drafts

Day Four
- personal writing
- further suggestions for revision

Day Five
- personal revisions

Day Six
- sharing second drafts
- debriefing the author group process

time commitment. Nonetheless, he agreed to try it, and we all agreed that the agenda was flexible based on our needs as a group and as individuals. Following is a summary of the group activity:

Day One: Each member of the group brainstormed alone for approximately three minutes. We then shared our ideas together in a round table meeting. This was a good opportunity to establish the way that the group would operate, including listening carefully to each person, ensuring contributions from all members of the group, providing positive feedback to one another, and framing suggestions as additional ideas for our writing.

After sharing our ideas as a group, we began to discuss in more detail which ideas we thought would make good narrative texts. As the discussion progressed, our ideas grew stronger, more developed, and more specific. One interesting result of this discussion is that members of the group began to borrow one another's ideas for themes and topics. Sarah, for example, joined her idea of a children's story with the theme of a child living at the side of the road in El Salvador (see Figure 3.2), an idea initially introduced by Connie. Connie combined two ideas and decided to highlight one anecdote from the family's travels and use it as the opening to a text about the overwhelming feeling of happiness one can experience in a given moment. Connor was intrigued by the idea of writing a story about a miniature underwater community, which was initially one of my ideas. After some interesting suggestions from all three of the other group members about what I could do with the theme of "what to do when you're waiting," I ended up going back to my first idea about the situation of working with a boy who had asked me for help in math class. The range of experiences of author group members gave me confidence that this story would appeal to a wide audience.

FIGURE 3.2
SARAH'S WORK: DAY ONE

Brainstorming List
- Poem about trip, 2 or 3 stanzas per place
- Story about Tortola—family, children's book with pictures and short story
- Probably children's story
- Bound book with wallpaper cover
- Blank paper and lined paper for story

(At)(The) Side of the Road
A day of a child living in Guatemala
- carrying baskets on their heads
- firewood
- living in their house (tin)
- bathroom
- traveler's perspective
- person perspective
- changes to people living it
- car driving by
- see people on the side of the road
- flashbacks
- some action
- children find fruit tree
- baskets on heads
- bargaining
- home with money

As a group, we discussed many areas of interest beyond the storylines we were developing. Connor wondered how people of the world ended up using so many different languages. We talked about how language began with early hominids and the mysterious process in which language shifted from being strictly representational to being a symbolic system used for creating thought and knowledge, and for metacognition. I worried about all this talk that did not directly relate to our writing. Reading Britton (1970) reassured me. He writes that talk is critical in the pursuit of new ideas. The new ideas can then feed into our writing and enrich the text.

The group decided that we needed some time to write down our initial ideas while they were fresh in our minds. At this point, all members of the author group sat at the same table and wrote. Some of us began to write immediately. Others thought about what they would write for approximately 10 more minutes before actually beginning to write. All four members of the group wrote for well over 30 minutes.

Day Two: Sarah shared her story with the group, indicating that she was not entirely happy with the way it was going (see Figure 3.3). Suggestions for Sarah included writing the story in the present tense instead of the past, providing more information about the main character, and making more overt the theme of living at the side of the road. I

FIGURE 3.3
SARAH'S WORK: DAY TWO

I walked over to meet Suzie at the fruit trees. It was the start of another day. My basket ring and empty basket were on my head. Suzie stood with her basket on the ground and was on her toes reaching up to pick the juicy mange off the tree. I walked over to a lime tree and started picking. After I had 10 or 12 I walked over to Suzie and we walked to the papaya tree. We picked some papayas and then placed our baskets on our heads and headed for the market. It was a long walk with the heavy basket weighing down my head and shoulders. The loud bustling about of the people in the market soon surrounded us. I had to walk very straight, holding my basket so that it wouldn't get knocked off. We found Mrs. Brown and set our baskets down beside her. People came to bargain with us and bought our fruit. The sun was hot so I sat in the shade of the trees and ate a mango, sucking the juice of and eating the fruit. It was very sweet, but quenched my thirst. I was very hungry still, though I always was.

remarked that Sarah's story seemed to have a cycle in it that began and ended "at the side of the road."

Connie was struggling with her story. She only shared the first paragraph, which described a moment with her family in Manuel Antonio National Park in Costa Rica. Suggestions for Connie included getting her ideas down on paper and then threading them together so they flowed as a natural series of thoughts and feelings. She also was encouraged to add more detail to her description of the moment in the park based on both the actual physical surroundings and the thoughts in her mind.

Connor shared his opening text, which set the stage for his story. It was a strong beginning, but he was not sure how to proceed. I suggested that he consider using a series of signposts (or boxes on paper) to map out the entire thread of the story so he had a plan of what to write about next.

I read to the group some passages of the text that I was working on. Connor and Connie suggested that I add more detail about the situation, the people involved, and my reaction to the situation.

At this point, we had an open discussion about the dangers of knowing one another so well and knowing the background of the stories we were writing. Sarah wondered if we were a good audience because of our familiarity. This made me think about the role of the author group in a new way. I believe that the primary function of the author group is not necessarily to be a first audience but to act as a support system in which knowing the details of the author's struggles allows us to provide one another with specific feedback. The author group also builds trust through sharing and support. Phenix (1990) identifies an additional purpose of the author group as an opportunity to look critically and analytically at writing, which in turn equips writers with the skills to look critically and analytically at their own writing. After this discussion, we each wrote independently for approximately 30 minutes and then met again to review our progress further.

Day Three: We began by writing and then followed up with a group discussion. Connie told us she was "fed up" with her piece and was avoiding writing. Connor mapped out his story in a series of boxes with arrows and moved on to writing the next section of the story. Sarah completed her first draft and started to "chunk" her story and rework some of her ideas (see Figure 3.4). I had written a very rough first draft and was adding more details. What struck me about the group was that we had developed a sense of collectivity in which the energy of the group pushed the individ-

---

FIGURE 3.4
SARAH'S WORK: DAY THREE

(continued from Day Two)
The afternoon was over and we left the market with an empty basket. I turned off the road to get to our house. Mother was washing the dishes when I gave her the money I'd earned
She gratefully pocketed it an gave me a kiss on the top of my head.
'Thanks dear' she said.
'Your welcome, mammy' I replied.
Dinner was small, as usual and we had beans, rice and tortillas. My stumach welcomed the food with a few grumbles.
I climbed into bed curled up into my corner of the house and fell asleep, shortly after dinner, preparing for another day in my mind.

---

uals to work harder. Two younger children in the house began writing in their journals at the same time that the author group met and wrote. The 4-year-old child mostly practiced writing his name, and the 7-year-old child recounted the day's activities with words and pictures. My brother-in-law joined us to listen as we shared our stories.

I noted that Connie's struggle through her writing was being shared with her own children. She admitted that this made her sympathetic toward her own children as writers. Connor agreed that it established an environment in which we are all learners together. This was particularly important because Connie had been Sarah and Connor's teacher for the previous seven months. Connie made a connection to a time recently when the three of them were learning Spanish in South America and they were all at the same level as learners in the same class. Connie said that it put them on an equal playing field because they were all learners.

Day Four: All four members of the group wrote this day; however, we concentrated on Connie's story. She found that her ideas did not flow well and asked for some help in making the pieces fit together. She read her story and received significant positive feedback. Each of the other three members of the group made specific suggestions about wording and the order of the sections. Connie immediately began to revise the text, taking out certain passages and making notes about what she would add. The other writers agreed to share their stories the next day. Sarah found that her story lacked the flavor of Guatemala and was not really a children's story like she wanted. She began to revise her story with short sentences and key words. Figure 3.5 shows Sarah's work on this day.

I observed that sometimes the attention focused on one writer in an author group meeting. Over time, we found it important that everyone had the opportunity to receive that same focused attention whether they were young or old, experienced writers or beginning writers.

Day Five: Sarah, Connor, and I shared our stories and remarked on the progress of each text. All members of the group provided specific feedback. I was initially concerned that Sarah and Connor would not participate in offering suggestions to Connie and me; however, after establishing the pattern of full participation by all group members, the suggestions were forthcoming and purposeful. The stories were well on their way to second draft stages. Figure 3.6 shows Sarah's progress.

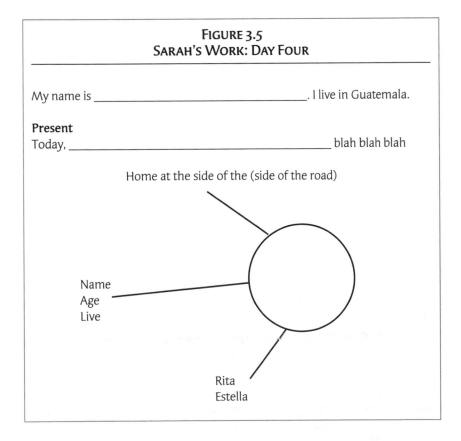

FIGURE 3.5
SARAH'S WORK: DAY FOUR

My name is _____. I live in Guatemala.

Present
Today, _____ blah blah blah

Home at the side of the (side of the road)

Name
Age
Live

Rita
Estella

Figure 3.6
Sarah's Work: Day Five

My name is Rita. I am 10 years old. I live in Guatemala with my mom and brothers and sisters in a small house at the side of the road. Each day I go to the market with my friend Estella, and we sell fruit with Señora Lopez.

I walk over and see Estella standing at the fruit trees. I have my basket ring and empty basket sitting on my head. Estella reaches up standing on her toes to pick a juicy mango off the tree. I walk over to a lime tree and start picking. I fill up my basket * and meet Estella at the road that leads to the market (*place it on my head).

We have a long walk along the side of the road to the market. My heavy basket weighs down my head and shoulders. Soon we are surrounded by the bustling around of the people in the market and I have to balance my basket on my head to make sure it doesn't get knocked off. We find Señora Lopez sitting in her stall and sit our baskets down beside her. People come to buy our fruit. The sun is hot, so I go sit under the shade of a tree and eat a mango. It's very sweet but tastes good. The afternoon is over, and we walk home with empty baskets.

When I see my house at the side of the road, I turn off and see mom waiting for me. I hand her the money I've earned and she pockets it with a kiss on top of my head. Dinner is small as usual. We have rice, beans, and tortillas. My stomach welcomes the food with a loud grumble. After dinner I curl up on the floor and fall asleep thinking about another day at the market. As my eyes close, I hear the sounds of dogs barking and people talking at the side of the road.

Day Six: The focus for this day was to debrief our experiences in the author group. I opened the discussion by describing my observation that everyone's ideas were listened to and respected. Sarah remarked that it was a positive group experience. Connie added that people can shut down when they are criticized in negative ways, and she was pleased at the positive approach we took. Each member of the group completed an evaluation form about the author group experience, and we decided that we wanted to gather a final copy of each story and bind them into a single collection. Questions continued to emerge as we worked on individual schedules to complete and edit our stories to each person's own satisfaction.

Our Findings

Each group member completed a short survey to rate our degree of satisfaction with the author group. From this survey we learned that the children, my sister, and I believe that the multiage author group is beneficial for writing and revisions. Connie highlighted the importance of making sure that the author group process is well thought out: "I think they are a fantastic idea but they must be set up very carefully." This is a critical observation. The author group will function effectively only when group members treat one another and their writing with respect and care. When I read Sarah's first draft and the progression to later drafts, the high quality of the revisions and the story generated is clearly evident. Personally, I believe that the quality of my writing improved tremendously through the constructive suggestions and feedback of group members, which combined with my own ideas, guided my revisions smoothly and naturally. Another example of quality improvement occurred through a discussion we had about using the past tense or the present tense and how it affects the stories. Sarah changed her story from the past tense to the present to make it seem more immediate and present. After seeing how it changed the feel of her story, I tried it myself. The text that I had been working on also changed dramatically when I switched to the present tense. It was as though the characters came to life in our stories.

Connie suggested that schools could conduct workshops for families to encourage family writing. She said, "I like the idea of family writing as a school activity, like 'Family Math' night; have a workshop to encourage family writing." Connor said, "I love the idea of talking to family." I do not anticipate that all families would enjoy writing together, but some may, as did the family of this case study.

We all felt that talking as a group is a very important feature of the writing process. Sarah said, "I really love the group working—especially the talks." In addition, we all believed that the group discussion helped us think about our own writing. Another indicator of the value of the discussions is the negotiation process that the group undertook to build additional meeting times into the schedule. On day two, for example, the group held two meetings on either side of a writing period.

We also saw the range of ages as a positive influence on the writing and on the group dynamics. Connie said, "I was impressed by the way the group was always respectful while offering lots of great constructive criticism. The age differences may have added depth to the group." We each brought our own perspective and experiences to the group. The questions we asked, seeking clarification about each other's writing, were genuine and allowed each of us to view our writing from other perspectives. For me, this interaction inspired playful creativity and a freshness in the use of words.

Key factors contributing to the success of this multiage author group include the following:

- the multiple ages and experience of group members,
- motivation of group members to write and revise their writing,
- respectful treatment of all members of the group,
- careful listening to one another's writing,
- an emphasis on positive and constructive criticism,
- establishing an expectation that all members will participate actively in discussions, and
- using specific guidelines for revising writing provided in the form of yes or no questions and short-answer responses that support the discussions and guide the writer through revisions.

The positive results of this multiage author group lead me to consider how the process might be replicated in the school setting. The nature of current school structures may make it difficult to find ways to group students of different classes and ages together for blocks of time. One way to approach it is to bring several interested teachers from different grades together and make groups from their classes. Another source of budding writers is the local high school. In many secondary schools, there are already programs in place in which students are given credit for working with students in elementary schools. This collaboration could be considered an enrichment experience or part of a work placement for higher achieving students. In addition, the Internet opens up possibilities for multiage author groups that extend beyond the classroom. The online mentoring relationships described in chapter 8 are an example of how writers of different ages can connect. In this case, secondary students read and provided feedback to younger students on their writing in an online format.

Another strategy is to invite parent volunteers or senior citizens from local centers to participate in multiage author groups. Connie is pursuing this idea in her children's schools. She is looking for the support of several volunteers and local principals in the same region. Her idea is that interested volunteer parents will work in pairs to facilitate multiage author groups. The groups will meet once or twice a week in one school, and the facilitators will meet regularly to discuss progress of the groups and their own writing struggles. The proposed members of the author groups will range in age from 9 years old to the adults volunteering to facilitate and participate in the groups. Connie will document the work and the results as a further development in the multiage author group story. This work may eventually lead to a model that can, in turn, be shared with other interested groups.

Conclusion

Multiage author groups provide some possible solutions to the ever-present knots we discover when we engage in the writing process and, even more critical, when we engage in sharing our writing with others for the purposes of revision. Revising one's own writing is still a difficult task, but with the support of other writers representing a broader spectrum of experience, I believe it can become more positive and effective. I am always hopeful when writers share fresh perspectives with other writers.

REFERENCES

Atwell, N. (1998). *In the middle: New understandings about writing, reading, and learning.* Portsmouth, NH: Boynton/Cook.

Britton, J. (1970). *Language and learning.* New York: Penguin.

Bruner, J.S. (1990). *Acts of meaning.* Cambridge, MA: Harvard University Press.

Graves, D.H. (1989). *The reading/writing teacher's companion: Experiment with fiction.* Portsmouth, NH: Heinemann.

Phenix, J. (1990). *Teaching writing: The nuts and bolts of running a day-to-day writing program.* Markham, ON: Pembroke.

Stake, R. (1995). *The art of case study research.* Thousand Oaks, CA: Sage.

Wells, G. (1999, November). *Dialogic inquiry in education.* Paper presented at the annual conference of the National Council of Teachers of English, Detroit, Michigan.

Wertsch, J., & Toma, C. (1995). Discourse and learning in the classroom: A sociocultural approach. In L.P. Steffe & J. Gale (Eds.), *Constructivism in education* (pp. 159–174). Hillsdale, NJ: Erlbaum.

CHAPTER 4

Untangling Knots in Early Writing: Young Children's Conceptions of Print

JANETTE PELLETIER AND JENNIFER LASENBY

What are the knots children encounter when they begin writing? What is it that we need to know about children's writing development in order to help them? These are questions of interest to many groups of stakeholders—parents, teachers, researchers, and children themselves. Are the knots, as Dyson (1995) summarizes, the graphics of the words, the link between signifier and signified, the actual process of writing, the genre, or the cultural event? We expect that all these factors are important as children begin to interact with print. In this chapter, we focus on how children come to link the signifier with the signified, that is, how they link what they write with what is meant. We take a psychological approach by examining young children's "theories" about print prior to their acquisition of the alphabetic principle. As young children first begin to write, their actions are guided by what they think print represents. Before they understand that the alphabet represents sounds, they use it in various ways that make sense to them. Based on our own research and that of others, we consider contexts and strategies for understanding and enhancing writing during early childhood, in the hope that understanding children's "conceptual knots" (i.e., what children think letters really represent) may lead to untangling them.

Why take children's theories as the starting point when thinking about how to help them untangle the knots in writing? Why not simply teach children to write following developmentally appropriate teaching practices? That is, provide children with wide-grip pencils and paper, and tell them to write and not to worry about spelling because spelling can be corrected later. The answer to this question lies in what makes sense to children. Increasingly, research is showing that young children growing up in "alphabetic societies" may, in fact, not use the alphabet at all when first looking at script and when using script themselves (Pelletier, 2002; Stanovich & Stanovich, 1998). This is true even in other alphabetic scripts that have different consonant-vowel systems, for example, Hebrew, which is strictly consonantal (Tolchinksy Landsman, 1990). Before any teaching begins, it is critical to observe what children do when they confront print, either in reading or in writing (Clay, 1982, 1991).

What do young children attend to in script if not the alphabet? Consider that their mission in life, since birth, is to look for patterns and to make sense of their world. As with anything else they encounter, children actively attempt to understand print and initially are faced with a significant knot—how to make sense of squiggles on a page that often, but not always, accompany an interesting picture. Children can use only knowledge and strategies that they have available for making meaning (Kress, 1996). When stories are read to them, children try to map what is meant onto the visual array of letters. To the young child, form and meaning are identical. However, the adult reading the story to the child is reading what is said by those very words (Olson & Pelletier, 2002). The words do, of course, convey meaning; however, what young children do not initially understand is that the printed words are representations of speech, that is, speech written down. In their minds, young children may see printed words only as representations of meaning and thus look for associations between the print and the object or event being described. This is an important distinction, one that children have to negotiate as they learn both to understand and to use alphabetic print, that is, to understand the difference between what is said and what is meant by the printed words. Let's consider a few examples from our research to highlight this point.

Research in Early Print Understanding

In a study of early print understanding with 66 children in the nursery school through grade 1 classes at our laboratory school at the Institute of Child Study, we show young children three words—*train, television, tea*—on a large white card. We ask them to point to the word *train*. For those children who have not yet considered the words as representations of speech, it is most likely that the word that most looks like a train will be the one they choose. Thus, they choose *television*. We ask, "Why did you choose that one?" They reply, "Because it's long." Another task involves presenting young children with the words *three little pigs*. Children repeat these three words. Then we cover up the last word and ask the children, "Now what does it say?" Again, children who are not yet aware of or able to use the alphabetic principle will employ some other strategy to answer this question. A common strategy that makes sense when the statement involves the number of pigs is to count the remaining marks on the card. In their minds, if the original number of marks separated by spaces said *three little pigs* and now there are only two separated by spaces, that must mean it now says *two little pigs*—a very clever misconception indeed (Pelletier, 2002)!

The examples in this study illustrate children's searches for pattern and order—how they untangle the knots in writing with the knowledge/information they have available. With this in mind, what do children do when they *produce* writing, rather than simply interpret it? Without an understanding of print as speech sounds, what would be the most obvious way to communicate in writing?

In an example provided by Kress (1997), a 4-year-old child wants to write that his daddy has a new car. He makes a circle shape representing *D* for the word *Daddy*, or...is it for the shape of the person, Daddy? He then makes more circles. Are these the letters *C, A, R* or are they the wheels of the new car? According to Kress, wheels may be as defining a feature of cars as letters are of the word *car*. As competent and practiced makers of signs, young children are trying to convey what is *meant*, not necessarily what is *said* by the very words, *Daddy has a new car.*

Consider another example. A 3-year-old girl wants to write *two horses*. She makes two circles, then one vertical line under each circle, followed by another vertical line under each circle. Finally she draws one horizontal line connecting the pairs of vertical lines. Are these vertical-horizontal line connections meant to represent *H* under each circle? Are they the legs and body of the objects, horses? When we observe her doing this, it is clear that she is giving each horse or word exactly the same treatment—she does two of everything. To look at the final product, we have a difficult time interpreting her story either logographically or alphabetically. However, she clearly is making meaning. She knows that she can use her pencil and paper to make a notation of two horses. The marks on the page could be letters, or they could be drawings. In her mind, they represent two horses. According to Kress (1997), the kinds of texts or speech genres that children bring to the learning of writing have a significant impact on how easily they are able to adapt to written communication. In this view, children who have more preschool exposure to written communication may find it easier to learn what writing signifies and how to use it in a relevant manner.

Furthermore, the children who may use their burgeoning understandings of letters as notation devices in one context may be just as apt to use scribble-writing in another context and drawings or letter-like drawings in another. To illustrate, 4-year-old Emily (all student names are pseudonyms) plays in the house center and writes out a lengthy shopping list. In this case, she chooses to use scribble-writing. Later that morning, Emily practices her letters by printing row after row of familiar letters, mostly those that appear in her name. The next day, the teacher asks Emily to write *Mommy has three apples*. Emily writes the word *Mom*, then writes the numeral *3*, followed by drawings of three apples (see Figure 4.1). Why does Emily take such different approaches in each of these contexts? Kress (1997) answers this question well:

> The learning of writing proceeds in exactly the same fashion as the development of other sign systems: employing the strategy of using the best, most apt available form for the expression of a particular meaning. Children use such representational means as they have available for making that meaning. (p. 17)

Imitation, instruction, construction—these are all ways in which Emily is learning to write. Learning by imitation occurs when observing her parents' cursive writing on the shopping list; Emily practices that in the house center. Learning by instruction occurs when she is explicitly taught how to form the letters of the alphabet. The teacher capitalizes on the children's interest in their own names; Emily practices that kind of writing at the writing center. Learning by construction occurs when Emily is given a challenge: Write *Mommy has three apples*. Emily has to use all representational means she has available to make meaning here. She can write some sight vocabulary and has practiced writing *MOM* before, and she can copy the numeral *3* from the number display in the class, but she does not know how to write *apples*, that is, she cannot "sound them out," so she draws them. But why draw three apples? She already has the number of apples encoded in the numeral *3*. With this action, Emily shows a budding understanding of syntax (numeral + object) but she overcompensates, want-

---

FIGURE 4.1
EMILY'S WRITING SAMPLE

ing to make sure she gets the message across that there are three apples. For Emily, what is meant is more important than what is said.

We ask Andrew, a 5-year-old boy in senior kindergarten, to write *Daddy has three hockey sticks*. He produces *Dady has tree holcke stik*. We see a significant difference between the 4- and 5-year-old children here. Andrew has acquired and is able to use the alphabetic principle in writing this sentence. So, how is his theory different from 4-year-old Emily's? The theory has changed from one in which print represents objects to one in which print now represents speech. Andrew is able to use his phonological understanding of the alphabet to sound out the utterance, map it onto the shapes of the letters he has learned to print, and separate each word with a space. Andrew no longer relies on the size, shape, or meaning of the object to write it down. He has learned to write because he has learned to use writing to represent the sounds of the words.

Having shown that even a single child will use different methods of writing to make the most sense in a given context, we nevertheless find it useful to know how, in general, children's most sophisticated strategy levels change over time. Are there developmental differences in the level of print representation when children are moving from drawings and scribbles to phonological processing, and are there differences in how children employ their naive theories as they try to untangle the knots? The following findings are taken from our ongoing longitudinal research study of children in our university laboratory school as they proceeded through the early grades from nursery (3-year-olds) to grade 1 (6-year-olds). We asked children to write the following, each on a separate page: *one cat, two horses, Mommy has four keys, Daddy has three hockey sticks,* and *[child's name] is [age] years old.*

We coded the children's written responses according to a developmental coding system that built on previous research (Tangel & Blachman, 1992) and was modified for our study. Specifically, as in previous research, we coded children's responses according to category level: No Response, Scribble, Drawing, Letter-Like Forms, Random Letters, Some Phonologically Correct Letters, and Correct Spelling. We coded children's writing of numbers as correct if their writing included the number of elements drawn or marked, or if they wrote the numeral itself. The results of the writing analysis reveal discrete gradations of emergent and early writing along a continuum rather than being limited to traditional categories typically found in early childhood curriculum guidelines (see Figure 4.2 for developmental differences).

Likewise, the number portion of the task shows clear developmental differences along the continuum (see Figure 4.3). That is, children are

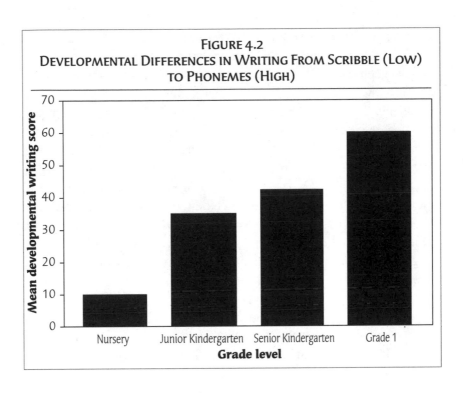

FIGURE 4.2
DEVELOPMENTAL DIFFERENCES IN WRITING FROM SCRIBBLE (LOW) TO PHONEMES (HIGH)

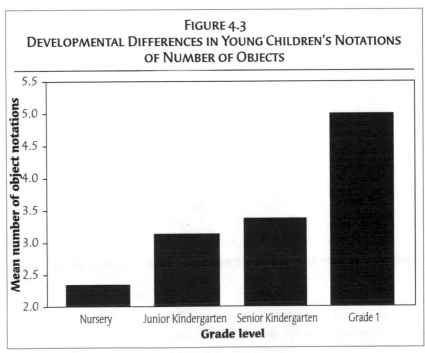

FIGURE 4.3
DEVELOPMENTAL DIFFERENCES IN YOUNG CHILDREN'S NOTATIONS OF NUMBER OF OBJECTS

increasingly able to use notation to record the number of objects either through correct number of items drawn or use of the actual numeral.

We gathered rich descriptions of children's reasoning as they applied their intuitive theories about print to their writing. For example, we asked 3-year-old Claire to write *Claire is three years old*. As she took her pencil, she made a thick vertical line and moved her pencil up and down over the line. She said, "Claire." She then made similar distinct marks for *is*, *three*, *years*, and *old*. Claire was making a mark for each word. Four-year-old Aaron wrote, *A A R O N • i 4 Z* and a picture of a hand with fingers to show his age. He used everything he knew to make his message clear. Although he did not know how to write *years old*, he was able to show his hand in print. Rather than a mark for each word, Aaron used words and letters for some words and pictures to represent objects, in this case, years. Five-year-old Jessica wrote *one cat* in the following way: *D A L*. For *two horses* Jessica wrote, *E* (backwards), *S S i C A L L E Y*. Jessica knew that two horses is more than one cat so she included more letters. Jessica used what she had available—the letters in her first and last name. She knew that "letters" make words but did not know which letters.

Implications for Teachers

In what ways can our research be of use to educators? Why do we think that understanding children's intuitive theories about print may be important to teaching writing? To begin, we hoped to underline the importance of two distinct ideas about young children's literacy development: (1) We need to understand children's intuitive theories about print so we know in what ways to challenge them, and (2) we need to acknowledge that children will not read or write fluently until they untangle the knots regarding the alphabet, specifically that words are sounds, not pictures of things. Thus, observation of children's early writing is critical to understanding what they think print is. Providing many opportunities for children to encounter print while learning the letter names, their sounds, and how to blend them will catapult children toward a way of thinking about text. And indeed, children need to "think about text" because when children have the idea that text is made up of the alphabet, and not pictures of things, the ambiguity about its meaning disappears. Children figure out that everyone can understand this universal printed language. They no longer think that the meaning is in the shape of the word or in the context cues; meaning becomes stable. So when children with this understanding write, they no longer need to ask, "What did I write?"

We end this chapter with some suggestions for parents and practitioners. Our main message has been to find out about children's theories of print and challenge those clever theories.

As Clay (1987) has claimed repeatedly, writing begins at home. If we think back to the three forms of learning that we outlined earlier—imitation, instruction, construction—we know that young children learn first from imitation (Olson & Bruner, 1996). Parents should model writing in the home and should talk about their writing as an intentional act; for example, "I am writing down all the things I need to get at the store"; "I am writing a letter to say hello to Grandma"; or "I am writing an e-mail message to Aunt Nancy." Parents might explain why they are writing a shopping list and what it says. They might model metalinguistic strategies, drawing attention to the terminology of writing, for example, "Let me finish this sentence. There's the period; that's the end of the sentence." Children naturally imitate adults in their culture and, if given writing tools, will soon begin to write themselves. We know from research that even very young children can distinguish drawings from writing (Clay, 1987; Ferreiro & Teberosky, 1979) and begin to make intentional marks on the page that represent this understanding. Drawing is not scribbling and writing is not drawing. Parents should express interest in children's writing, ask questions, and encourage children to use writing for a communicative purpose.

An important message for parents is to allow their children to write without correction. Deliberate attempts to teach children to succeed may cause them to avoid print-related activities (Clay, 1987). Some families feel compelled to prepare their young children for school in ways that emphasize too strongly the need for correctness. Their well-intentioned tutoring and expectations for practice may, in fact, limit their children's willingness to explore the properties of print in meaningful ways. Thus, families should be encouraged to allow their children to play with print, observe the properties of text, and make the discovery of what print represents.

Teachers of young children can facilitate this discovery. They should always start with careful observation—the "child study" approach to teaching. Clay has numerous assessment tools appropriate for understanding children's awareness of print in the early years classroom (see, for example, Clay, 1991, for discussion of her concepts about print). According to Clay, teachers should use these assessments to modify literacy instruction for individual children.

Furthermore, our own research points to the usefulness of tasks that challenge children to untangle referential writing from phonetic writing. Referential writing involves writing words in a way that relates to the features of the referent (writing *snake* with more signs than *butterfly* because a snake is longer). We want children to untangle this important knot; they must come to see that shape and size are not related to sound and that words are made of sounds. We want children to be active constructors of print knowledge rather than passive recipients of our instruction. In psychological terms, we want to throw children's previous theories (print = objects) into disequilibrium until the new evidence (print = words) becomes assimilated into their thinking (words = sounds). Children who are more advanced along the writing continuum in kindergarten are better readers in grade 1. The experience in writing itself contributes to children's ability to decode and understand text.

In this way, teachers are able to respond positively to children's initial writing attempts and encourage children in their experimentation with print. Teachers should serve as models for literate behavior by providing opportunities for children to observe them reading and writing. Teachers also can encourage children to use print to support oral language activity and dramatic play by having a variety of writing tools available within children's reach. For example, teachers can leave phone message pads, envelopes, notepads, and cardboard in the dramatic play area for children to write phone messages, restaurant orders, menus, and letters. They can allow children to dictate stories, retell familiar stories, write scripts, and engage in drama and puppetry. Teachers can invite children to record their personal experiences, dictated words, and stories in daily or weekly journal entries. They also can use literacy albums for name-writing attempts; audiotapes of pretend storybook readings; photographs of play constructions with child comments; drawings with dictated stories; lists of favorite books, authors, or words; special scribble messages (invitations, letters); parent anecdotes about home literacy or special stories; and teachers' anecdotal observations, along with photographs of children engaged in writing.

Certainly these more holistic approaches to supporting writing play an important role in an early years class. Teachers can show that they value children's writing by collecting their written pieces, having discussions about their writing, sharing books written by children, and encouraging children to call themselves writers (Graves, 1991). Exposure to literate environments alone can account for some aspects of children's reading development (Cunningham & Stanovich, 1993, 1998). New computer-linked networks provide an example of meaningful communication using technology (Scardamalia, Bereiter, & Lamon, 1994). Imagine first-grade scientists e-mailing entomologists with their observations of how classroom roaches breathe. Children who have difficulty holding a writing tool may be more motivated to write via a computer keyboard or to use plastic letters to form words. Classrooms can reflect rich literacy experiences that children may have outside school by having signs, labels, magazines, recipes, and similar items available.

Teacher manuals and textbooks offer strategies for motivating children to write in kindergarten and at home. For example, Heller (1996) suggests that children should have opportunities to (1) write about activities that matter to them personally; (2) write about things they have experienced; (3) write about familiar persons, places, or things; and (4) write in response to children's literature. She also advocates that teachers encourage parents to support classroom instruction by taking time to talk and listen to their children, use read-alouds at every opportunity, write with their children, and display their writing in their home environment.

All these suggestions are important. However, the key point that we hope to make in this chapter is that merely being provided the opportunity to write and being supported in efforts to write may not be enough for many children. Children who persist in their early theories may have significant writing knots to untangle if those theories go unchallenged. It is important that they come to see print as words and to see that words are composed of the sounds of the alphabet. Research has given us that knowledge. Good teachers can take it from there.

REFERENCES

Clay, M.M. (1982). *Observing young readers*. Portsmouth, NH: Heinemann.

Clay, M.M. (1987). *Writing begins at home: Preparing children for writing before they go to school.* Portsmouth, NH: Heinemann.

Clay, M.M. (1991). *Becoming literate: The construction of inner control*. Portsmouth, NH: Heinemann.

Cunningham, A., & Stanovich, K. (1993). Children's literacy environments and early word recognition. In *Reading and Writing. Special Issue: The role of decoding in reading research and instruction, 5*(2), 193–204.

Cunningham, A., & Stanovich, K. (1998). The impact of print exposure on word recognition. In J. Metsala & L. Ehri (Eds.), *Word recognition in beginning literacy* (pp. 235–262). Mahwah, NJ: Erlbaum.

Dyson, A.H. (1995). *Children out of bounds: The power of case studies in expanding visions of literacy development* (Tech. Rep. No. 73). Berkeley, CA: National Center for the Study of Writing.

Ferreiro, E., & Teberosky, A. (1979). *Literacy before schooling*. Portsmouth, NH: Heinemann.

Graves, D.H. (1991). *Build a literate classroom*. Portsmouth, NH: Heinemann.

Heller, M.F. (1996). *Reading-writing connections: From theory to practice.* White Plains, NY: Longman.

Kress, G. (1996). Writing and learning to write. In D. Olson & N. Torrance (Eds.), *The handbook of education and human development: New models of learning, teaching and schooling* (pp. 225–256). Oxford, UK: Blackwell.

Kress, G. (1997). *Before writing: Rethinking the paths to literacy.* New York: Routledge.

Olson, D., & Bruner, J. (1996). Folk psychology and folk pedagogy. In D. Olson & N. Torrance (Eds.), *The handbook of education and human development: New models of learning, teaching and schooling* (pp. 9–27). Oxford, UK: Blackwell.

Olson, D., & Pelletier, J. (2002). Schooling and the development of literacy. In K. Connelly & J. Valsiner (Eds.), *The handbook of developmental psychology* (pp. 358–369). London: Sage.

Pelletier, J. (2002). Children's "clever misunderstandings" about print. In J. Brockmeier, M. Wang, & D. Olson (Eds.), *Literacy, narrative and culture* (pp. 245–265). Surrey, UK: Curzon Press.

Scardamalia, M., Bereiter, C., & Lamon, M. (1994). The CSILE project: Trying to bring the classroom into World 3. In K. McGilly (Ed.), *Classroom lessons: Integrating cognitive theory and classroom practice* (pp. 201–228). Cambridge, MA: MIT Press.

Stanovich, K., & Stanovich, P. (1998). Ending the reading wars. *Orbit, 28*(4), 49–55.

Tangel, D.M., & Blachman, B.A. (1992). Effect of phoneme awareness instruction on kindergarten children's invented spelling. *Journal of Reading Behavior, 24*(2), 233–261.

Tolchinsky Landsman, L. (1990). Literacy development and pedagogical implications: Evidence from the Hebrew system of writing. In Y. Goodman (Ed.), *How children construct literacy: Piagetian perspectives* (pp. 26–44). Newark, DE: International Reading Association.

Diversity and Teaching Writing

IN THIS SECTION, we move from discussions of more mainstream issues in teaching writing to those that address the diversity found in many contemporary classrooms. The challenges in helping children write in a second language are addressed in chapters 5 and 6. In chapter 5, Monika Smith and Donald S. Qi examine some of the difficulties faced by English language learners (ELLs) and their teachers, looking at language issues as well as social and culture issues. While underlining the complexity of the knot of teaching writing to ELL students in the mainstream classroom, Monika and Donald offer numerous suggestions for instruction and assessment. They emphasize the need to view ELL students not as a knot to be untangled but as a "resource to be cherished." In chapter 6, Sharon Lapkin describes a procedure—reformulation—that helps second language students move toward native speaker levels in their grammar, vocabulary, and spelling. Drawing from her research with French immersion students, she proposes that use of the reformulation strategy, together with student collaboration and some teacher intervention, provides second language students with opportunities to try out their growing knowledge of grammar and vocabulary in the target language. In addition, students benefit from receiving native speakers' feedback on their writing.

In chapter 7, Shelley Peterson addresses the gender disparity that has been highlighted in reports of large-scale writing test scores. She discusses the results of research examining teachers' perceptions of boys' and girls' writing and offers suggestions for teachers to begin untangling an issue that has not traditionally been identified as a knot. These suggestions involve raising awareness of gender perceptions, reflecting on and modifying feedback provided to girls and boys about their writing, and adding new criteria to rubrics used to assess students' writing.

CHAPTER 5

A Complex Tangle: Teaching Writing to English Language Learners in the Mainstream Classroom

MONIKA SMITH AND DONALD S. QI

Let us take a look at one of today's multicultural classrooms: In a U.S. grade 3 science class, students have been measuring the growth of bean sprouts under different watering conditions. Now they are to write a report on their findings. The students are chatting in groups about what they want to include in their writing. One group has an older student who is clearly not a native speaker of English but who is communicating quite fluently with the other students. He has observed carefully and contributes good ideas to his group's project. However, when the other students begin to write, he draws pictures of the plants. The only writing he does is the labeling of some items in his drawing.

What is going on here? If the student speaks so fluently, why can't he write? Does he have a learning disability? No. However, he has only been in the United States for one year. He came as a refugee from a war-torn country in which his schooling had been interrupted for some time. Since his arrival in the United States, he has been trying to catch up and has managed to learn a lot of conversational English. But, a more cognitively demanding task such as report writing is still well beyond his capabilities.

This student's case is by no means unusual. Several English as a second language (ESL) and mainstream teachers have reported to us that English language learners (ELLs) sit separately and draw pictures while the rest of the class is engaged in writing. Indeed, using drawings to overcome obstacles and express meanings is often a strategy proposed for ELL students at an early stage of their writing development (Cloud, Genesee, & Hamayan, 2000; O'Malley & Pierce, 1996). But, as one teacher asked us recently, "How many pictures can a student draw and label?" Drawing and labeling will not contribute to a great extent to the development of grammatical and discourse skills that are essential to writing. At some stage, these skills need to be addressed, and the student will have to produce not just oral but written output.

Clearly, ELL students have to learn to write in English and to speak the language. Some are lucky enough to get extra help with producing written texts in ESL pull-out programs. But for many, the mainstream classroom is the only place where they are taught to write. Their classmates, for whom English is the mother tongue, will already have substantial knowledge of English vocabulary and sentence structures when they begin writing. They will continue to improve their writing skills while the ELL students struggle to learn the language at the same time as they are learning to write. Their teachers struggle to teach them without neglecting their other students. How can ELL students catch up to their classmates? What can be done?

The multiple problems faced by ELL students in the mainstream classroom when it comes to writing are not always obvious, and neither are the causes for these problems. The knot that impedes smooth development of writing skills becomes a tangle comprised of many strands, and many pins are needed for isolating the strands and beginning to unpick the tangle. This chapter looks at some of the strands that make up the tangle and at some of the pins that may help teachers deal with the situation.

The Strands Untangled

We divide the strands into two major types: those of the learners and those of the teachers.

The Learners

Language Issues. Our first strand has to do with the students' proficiency in English. Obviously, students will not be able to write in a language that they do not know. But, as we have already seen, many ELL students learn to speak English fairly quickly to a reasonable standard. They can communicate with their teachers and their classmates, they can understand and follow basic instructions, and they may be able to ask for help if they are stuck. Why is writing so much harder for ELL students to learn than speaking?

Cummins (2001) distinguishes three "faces" of language proficiency: conversational fluency, discrete language skills, and academic language proficiency. ELL students generally develop conversational fluency fairly quickly. This is the ability to hold one's own in a conversation on familiar topics, using high-frequency words and simple grammatical structures with the support of gestures, intonations, and facial expressions. Discrete language skills are acquired through direct instruction and practice, such as in reading. The skills include recognizing the alphabet and decoding written words. Again, most ELL students manage to pick up the alphabet reasonably quickly once they begin schooling in English. But, decoding individual words is not the same as understanding the whole text. A student who reads fairly fluently may have only a vague idea of a text's contents. Writing is even more complex because it requires, in addition to the previously mentioned skills, academic language proficiency, which is not learned as quickly or as easily as the other two skills. According to Cummins (2001),

> Academic language proficiency includes knowledge of the less frequent vocabulary of English as well as the ability to interpret and produce increasingly complex written (and oral) language. As students progress through the grades, they encounter far more low frequency words (primarily from Greek and Latin sources), complex syntax (e.g. passives), and abstract expressions that are virtually never heard in everyday conversation. Students are required to understand linguistically and conceptually demanding texts in the content areas (e.g. literature, social studies, science, mathematics) and to use this language in an accurate and coherent way in their own writing. (p. 65)

Indeed, writing is not just the act of setting down spoken sentences on paper but an entirely separate skill. However, the differences between the three previously mentioned types of language skills often are not recognized by planners of educational policies or curricula, or by the general public. They forget that everyday conversation consists mostly of short, disjointed phrases and employs a limited amount of vocabulary; that people do not normally speak in well-planned and constructed paragraphs; and that repetition is common in conversation. Consequently, ELL students who can speak reasonably fluently and who have learned basic language skills are expected to be equally proficient in the academic language skill. And, when these students fail to learn to write as quickly as their English speaking classmates, they may come to be regarded as less intelligent or as "language disabled" and are likely to be subjected to "mismatched interventions" (Poplin & Phillips, 1993). We have already seen an example of this in the mainstream classroom: A student may be given a simplified task such as drawing a picture rather than being given the extra time and special help needed for learning to write a description of a science experiment. Picture labeling can be a useful simplification of a writing task if it has no more purpose than the teaching of discrete language skills or if it is seen as an alternative means of assessing the student's subject knowledge. Development of the student's academic language proficiency will not be aided in this way.

However, it needs to be noted that, although academic proficiency is distinct from the other two language skills, the role of conversational fluency and discrete language skills in the development of the academic proficiency must not be ignored either. In fact, many ELL students do struggle with basic conversational fluency and with discrete language skills. Consequently, they lack basic vocabulary and syntactic structures as well as knowledge of the elements essential to the English writing system. Also, acquiring discrete language skills such as learning the alphabet is harder for ELL students whose mother tongue is exclusively oral or has a different (e.g., logographic) writing system. Learning to form letters may be awkward for such students and slow them down considerably. Thus, efforts also must be made to improve ELLs' conversational fluency and discrete language skills in order to make the skills serve as useful tools to facilitate the process of developing writing.

Writing conventions also can differ greatly among languages and cultures. For instance, a Japanese student's failure to begin a letter by naming the addressee can be due to Japanese formal letter-writing conventions (the addressee is often mentioned only at the end of the letter) rather than lack of English language proficiency. Thus, it cannot be assumed that ELL students who are already literate in their mother tongues automatically have knowledge of English discourse features or literary genres. When these are taught in the mainstream classroom, ELL students may need to unlearn old writing conventions at the same time as they learn the new English ones. This makes the task much harder for them than for their English-speaking classmates.

While the students' mother tongue may sometimes interfere with their acquisition of English, it is generally more of a help than a hindrance (Cummins, 2001). For students who have already learned to write in their own language, writing skills in the mother tongue can carry over into writing in English (Cumming, 1989). Sometimes basic elements in the first language parallel complex elements of English. For instance, students from romance language backgrounds such as Spanish can have an advantage over their English-speaking classmates when it comes to learning Latin-based, low-frequency vocabulary in the English language (Cummins, 2001).

In short, when language issues relating to ELL students are to be understood and addressed in mainstream classrooms, it is important to distinguish the functions, as well as to recognize the relationships, of the three different faces of language proficiency vis-à-vis writing development. It is also necessary that the features of the students' first language be taken into account in this process.

Social and Cultural Issues. Apart from specific language problems, ELL students also face social problems in the English-speaking environment (Cummins, 2001). They have to learn to fit into the culture of a new country and classroom. This can lead to a number of conflicts that are not necessarily obvious. For example, schools (re)construct their students' identities. Hunter (1997) describes how an ELL student learning to write also learns to adopt a new identity as an insider in his new peer group. This new identity clashes with his earlier identity as a "good student" meeting the teacher's and his parents' expectations. Consequently, the student's literacy skills development experiences a setback.

The English-speaking world is based on literacy, and the value of reading and writing is taken for granted. However, learning styles can differ widely among cultures, and not all cultures are literate or accord such a high value to literacy. Masny and Ghahremani-Ghajar (1999) discuss this point in their ethnographic case study of Somalian children in Canadian primary schools. The Somalian students' home culture embraces several different kinds of literacies: home-based, religious, and school-based. While religious-based literacy stresses reading and memorization of sections of the Koran, Somalian home traditions stress oral communication over reading, and telephone conversations are preferred to letter writing. For these students, learning to write at a Canadian school will mean having to simultaneously adopt new forms of communication.

Home help with writing assignments may not be as available to the ELL students as it is to their English-speaking classmates. Immigrant parents often struggle with the new language of their adopted country and may themselves have trouble with producing academic writing in English. Although they are likely to be more literate in their mother tongue than their children, the parents may not see writing in the mother tongue as important for their children. Sakamoto (2000) shows that immigrant parents are likely to stress speaking and listening for meaningful communication with their children but that writing and reading are not actively pursued at home.

The above issues become highly relevant when we look at the writing tasks and assignments our ELL students are given. Some assignments may be culturally inappropriate or use the wrong level of intimacy. For instance, teachers may attempt to make the writing task more relevant to their students by asking questions that are regarded as too personal in the children's own culture and that they feel uncomfortable answering. In some cultures, stating a personal opinion or arguing a case in opposition to an older person's opinion is regarded as drawing undue attention to oneself. Instead, students are expected to write down, sometimes verbatim, what they have been told by the teacher or read in a textbook. ELL students from such cultures may have great difficulties composing an opinion piece or original work.

The Teachers

Teaching ELL students presents challenges to teachers, as well as to students. In dealing with ELL students in a mainstream classroom, teachers are expected to act as language teachers, often without adequate knowledge, training, preparation, or materials. At the same time, they need to teach the standard curriculum to the whole class. Teachers may not be able to tell, without specialist training, how to provide appropriate scaffolding and intellectual challenges to individual ELL students or how to prepare these students for their writing tasks. They may assume knowledge where it is not present. On the other hand, teachers also may underestimate the students' knowledge because of language difficulties. How do teachers tell if ELL students have understood their explanations when they have communication difficulties?

Many schools lack the appropriate support systems to help teachers cope with ELL students in the mainstream. If ESL and pull-out programs are available, they are often exclusively geared toward helping beginners become reasonably fluent in English. Once the students have acquired the deceptive basic interpersonal communicative skills (BICS, described fully in Cummins, 2001)—that is, once they are able to talk with their classmates and to understand their teachers' instructions—they are deemed to have caught up with their classmates. They are then fully integrated in the mainstream long before they have acquired the cognitive academic language proficiency (CALP) (Cummins, 2001) that they need to function successfully in highly cognitive tasks. Writing is the most common of these tasks and pervades all levels of teaching and learning in the North

American classroom environment. Many ELL students, because of misguided and misinformed policies or insufficient financial support, are integrated into mainstream classrooms from the start of their schooling in the English-speaking environment. It may be possible to pay extra attention to just one ELL student in the classroom, but what if several have to be integrated at once? The more ELL students there are in a mainstream classroom, the less time the teacher will have to provide individual support to each of those students while keeping their standard curriculum running at the same time.

We have mentioned earlier that insufficient language proficiency can be misdiagnosed as a learning disability. Of course, the opposite is also possible. An existing learning disability may be masked by the student's poor English. A generalized needs analysis may not necessarily pick up problems specific to the ELL student's writing proficiency. If no specialized needs assessment for ELL students is available, teachers may not be able to determine whether students are struggling in the classroom because of language, social/cultural, or disability problems, or because of insufficient or interrupted prior schooling in their home countries.

The strands of the teacher's tangle are comprised of learner issues, both linguistic and cultural, as well as teacher issues arising from insufficient training and lack of a supportive infrastructure, including lack of financial support and appropriate teaching materials, and misguided educational policies.

Finding the Pins

What can be done? How can teachers help ELL students learn how to write in English and cope with writing tasks? Both learners and teachers need pins to isolate the strands that make up the tangle and to untangle at least some of its snarls. In the next section we discuss some of the pins.

Helping the Learners

Using the Students' Mother Tongue. First, teachers need to be aware of the language problem and possible root causes of it. For example, if students have adequate writing skills in their mother tongue but lack sufficient English vocabulary, then teaching the students to use graphic organizers to plan a writing task is not likely to be successful, unless the students also have access to a bilingual dictionary. ELL students can be aided by special one-on-one attention, by being given sequential, additional preparatory instructions beyond those that are offered to their English-speaking classmates. These instructions may be offered through individualized instructional packages, through the use of alternatives to writing, and through special assessment. But, this close attention to ELL students may not be useful if it does not address the underlying cause of an individual student's problem. Therefore, a detailed needs assessment is absolutely necessary to determine what individual attention and help is likely to be most beneficial for ELL students. If a student's English is poor, such an assessment may not be possible in English and will have to be conducted, if at all possible, in the student's mother tongue instead.

In addition to assessment, it may be useful to include the students' mother tongue in some classroom tasks. Foreign and second language writing research demonstrates that students' ability to write in their mother tongues is a valuable asset to English writing development and can contribute directly to success in English writing tasks. Examples of such tasks are writing a text in the mother tongue before translating it into English (Kobayashi & Rinnert, 1992) and mental translation (Qi, 1998). In the latter case, students, while composing directly in English, often think of a word in their mother tongue before translating it into English. For example, in Qi's study, the student first came up with the word *rationally* in her mother tongue and then translated it into English before incorporating it into her written text. Thus, a priority for any teacher faced with ELL students in the mainstream class must be to set up a support network for those students (and the teachers themselves) that utilizes the students' mother tongues. Cummins' (2001) linguistic interdependence principle suggests that instruction that develops children's mother tongue reading and writing skills is not just developing those mother tongue skills but also "a deeper conceptual and linguistic proficiency that is strongly related to the development of literacy in the majority language" (p. 174).

Although teachers cannot be expected to know all their students' mother tongues, it is a great advantage if they can communicate with students in their mother tongue at least some of the time. Help in the mother tongue also can be provided by bilingual colleagues, parents, outside tutors, or peers who share the ELL students' languages. Peer help can be especially valuable not only for the struggling ELL students but also for the more experienced helpers themselves because teaching something is often the best way to learn it. However, peer help can carry its own problems. The following tale from a grade 6 teacher sounds a necessary note of caution:

> Last year I had a student who spoke [the student's mother tongue] and no English. I was pleased that there was another girl in the class who spoke [the mother tongue] and could translate for X. However, it didn't take long to realize that things weren't going well. The other girl was desperate to feel accepted by some of the more popular girls in the class, and helping poor X (whose clothes and weight did not conform to the dominant definition of "cool") was not in her game plan. I talked to her a little about the pressure she was putting on herself to be popular but, nevertheless, stopped asking her to help X. (E. Haas, personal communication, March 19, 2002)

Still, as we have mentioned above, teachers cannot be expected to provide constant special attention to their ELL students either. Outside help may be needed. If no special tutors or other teachers' helpers are available, it is time to call on the students' ethnic community. Parents are a most valuable source of help and may be willing to provide some help both inside and outside the classroom, especially for supporting the students' mother tongue development. An exciting example for this is the Pajaro Valley project (Ada, 1988) in which Spanish-speaking parents living in and near Watsonville, California, helped and motivated their children to read and write in their own language by reading Spanish books to them or by reading aloud the children's writing on a local television program. The students' developing interest in literacy skills in their mother tongue positively affected their English writing.

Writing in English. As mentioned before, alternatives to writing—such as drawing and labeling; copying words, sentences, and paragraphs; filling in charts and worksheets; giving an oral presentation in place of a written report; or acting out a topic—can be used at the beginning of writing instruction. Adaptations must not stop here, however. Those alternatives make relatively few cognitive demands on language users. There is a huge difference between writing single words or short sentences and producing complex sentences, paragraphs, and longer texts. In order to develop the language skills required for functioning in the academic environment, students need to learn and practice this kind of complex writing, which requires much more cognitive involvement. In addition, they need to become familiar with different writing conventions and genres.

Dialogue journals (O'Malley & Pierce, 1996; Peyton & Reed, 1990) are one way of developing this expertise. Students choose the topic about which they want to write and enter into a written dialogue with their teacher. The students' writing is not corrected or evaluated in any way, but the teacher's responses and questions provide a model for writing.

However, ELL students also need to be able to cope with given topics and assignments. The student from the introduction to this chapter, who has been drawing bean sprouts, needs to learn to describe the sprouts' growth as well as depict it. He could, for instance, work with a model of a scientific report, which introduces him to sentence patterns to be imitated. Or, the teacher could reformulate the student's report so it conforms more closely to standard expectations. Like dialogue journals, reformulation (Cohen, 1989; see also chapter 6) provides a model for writing that can help students evaluate their own performance and compare it to an English standard. This approach is especially useful for improving students' language skills. In reformulation, a native speaker of English rewrites the ELL student's work in the way a native speaker would have expressed it but does not change the contents. The ELL student is then given an opportunity to compare the original piece of writing with its reformulation and to notice differences.

Cummins (2001) suggests using a special type of reformulation, to be performed by the students themselves. ELL students' writing in the mother tongue is translated by a computer translation program, such as Systran's Babel Fish (http://babelfish.altavista.com). Computer translations are notoriously inadequate, but they can at least give some indications of text contents. Then the ELL students and their classmates, individually or in collaboration with the whole class, can work out what the computer translation program has been trying to express and provide their own version in correct English. Such an exercise is not only valuable for improving the ELL students' language skills, but it also gives the whole class, including the ELL students, a chance to work together on a writing task in which even the students with lower English proficiency contribute equally. In fact, as the ELL students have supplied the original contents of the writing text with which the rest of the class then engages, they become important members of the classroom community and have the feeling that their contributions are of value, which is a tremendous confidence booster.

Another way to empower the students' own culture and production is to publish or display their work—maybe both in the original language version and in translation—on the classroom bulletin board, in the class newspaper, or in other ways, with guidance, editing, and help from the teacher or English-speaking peers, if necessary. Sangwine (1988) finds that her classroom publication projects greatly motivate her students. For the projects, immigrant students write about their life experiences in the new country, assemble the written pieces together in the form of a book, and then circulate this book among the senior citizens in a local community. Like published writers, the students engage in exploring an interesting subject and writing for a real audience, and they find satisfaction through the steps of discovering what they want to say about their experiences.

One-on-one writing conferences between teachers and learners provide excellent opportunities to attend to those specific areas that need more attention. However, teachers here need to be sensitive to two issues. First, we already have seen that offering an ELL student additional instructions and treatments different from the rest of the class also can create its own problems. If ELL students are keen to adapt to the classroom culture, then any attempt to give them extra help (e.g., different assignments, more time to finish a test, etc.) can be perceived as "singling out" and be taken to indicate that the students do not "fit in." As our earlier anecdote about peer help shows, the same can be true for the more proficient ethnic peer. Second, whether they are talking to ELL students in the classroom or in separate conferences, teachers need to be careful to listen to their students and to observe their own behavior in these interactions. Verplaetse (1998) shows that teachers unwittingly tend to ask far fewer questions and to issue far more directives in interactions with students with limited English proficiency than with their English-speaking classmates. This modification of teacher talk can reduce ELL students' opportunities to create language output and to improve their language skills.

Assessing ELL Writing

When assessing ELL students' writing, it is necessary to look at the purpose of the writing task. In ESL classes, writing is often practiced with the specific purpose of using the foreign or second language as the object of the task. Most attention is given to the question of whether the language is used correctly and appropriately, and assessment is based on the number of linguistic errors made. Content may be of secondary importance. The teacher will be less concerned with what the students write about than whether they write about it correctly.

In the mainstream writing classroom, language is the tool for expressing the text's message and content. Discourse features may become more important than the language that is used to express them. Because

English is a foreign language to ELL writers, they need to reconcile both aspects of the language in their writing, and teachers need to be aware of this and make allowances where necessary. Superficial errors, such as faulty spelling or grammar, are very noticeable and can easily draw the teacher's attention away from the other merits of a piece of writing, such as sincere attempts to pay close attention to the topic or to express a complex point with limited vocabulary.

O'Malley and Pierce (1996) suggest that teachers keep in mind the following important points when assessing ELL writers' performance:

- assess stages of writing development, writing processes, and strategies as well as the final product;
- assess writing in context with other language skills;
- assess all domains of writing, not just language mechanics;
- include self-assessment of writing and involve students in setting assessment criteria and creating and selecting writing prompts;
- use multiple assessment across a variety of purposes, genres, and content areas;
- use portfolios to show progress over time; and
- use the results of writing assessments and of teachers' conferences with the students to plan instruction. (p. 160)

A writing portfolio gives the teacher a chance to assess students' progress in the various areas listed, measuring performance over the year rather than comparing it to an English standard set from outside the classroom.

In summary, the pins that can help isolate some of the strands of the tangle involve teachers' use of a variety of instructional and assessment resources to help ELL students. These include

- making efforts to understand the underlying causes of the problem;
- capitalizing on the students' mother tongue for assessing students' existing literacy abilities and for offering instructional support;
- using tasks that effectively help ELL students improve their English writing quality; and
- giving additional individual assistance as well as conducting comprehensive and instrumental assessment of ELL writing with a view to promoting future English writing development.

Conclusions

At the very least, the teaching of writing to ELL students in the mainstream classroom means a lot of extra work for the teacher. For effective instruction to take place, teachers must be aware of the complexity of the tangle. The issues and proposed methods and resources described and discussed in this chapter merely present a sample of the many complex issues at stake. Teachers cannot and should not be expected to act as language teachers without training. Such training needs to include components of language (ESL) teaching methodology and cultural awareness and to address the issues specific to ELL students and the conditions that can promote their literacy development.

We have seen teaching and assessing ELL students' writing as a highly complex problem that is not easily resolved. However, many ELL students do learn to write successfully in English. They may have somewhat idiosyncratic ways of going about the writing task, but they also contribute new experiences and ideas to the mainstream classroom. In this way, ELL students can be seen not as a problem to be solved but as a resource to be cherished.

NOTE: The authors would like to thank Shelley Peterson, Shosh Brenner, Ruth Coulter, Mary Godwin, Elizabeth Haas, and Lisbeth Paisley-Smith for their helpful input into this chapter.

REFERENCES

Ada, A.F. (1988). The Pajaro Valley experience: Working with Spanish-speaking parents to develop children's reading and writing skills in the home through the use of children's literature. In T. Skutnabb-Kangas & J. Cummins (Eds.), *Minority education: From shame to struggle* (pp. 223–238). Clevedon, UK: Multilingual Matters.

Cloud, N., Genesee, F., & Hamayan, E. (2000). *Dual language instruction: A handbook for enriched education.* Boston: Heinle & Heinle.

Cohen, A.D. (1989). Reformulation: A technique for providing advanced feedback in writing. *Guidelines: A Periodical for Classroom Language Teachers, 11*(2), 1–9.

Cumming, A. (1989). Writing expertise and second language proficiency. *Language Learning, 39,* 81–141.

Cummins, J. (2001). *Negotiating identities: Education for empowerment in a diverse society* (2nd ed.). Ontario, CA: California Association for Bilingual Education.

Hunter, J. (1997). Multiple perceptions: Social identity in a multilingual elementary classroom. *TESOL Quarterly, 31*(3), 603–611.

Kobayashi, S., & Rinnert, C. (1992). Effects of first language on second language writing: Translation versus direct composition. *Language Learning, 42,* 183–215.

Masny, D., & Ghahremani-Ghajar, S. (1999). Weaving multiple literacies: Somali children and their teachers in the context of school culture. *Language, Culture and Curriculum, 12*(1), 72–93.

O'Malley, J.M., & Pierce, L.V. (1996). *Authentic assessment for English language learners*. Reading, MA: Addison-Wesley.

Peyton, J.K., & Reed, L. (1990). *Dialogue journal writing with non-native English speakers: A handbook for teachers*. Alexandria, VA: Teachers of English to Speakers of Other Languages.

Poplin, M., & Phillips, L. (1993). Sociocultural aspects of language and literacy: Issues facing educators of students with learning disabilities. *Learning Disability Quarterly, 16*, 245–255.

Qi, D.S. (1998). An inquiry into language-switching in second language composing processes. *Canadian Modern Language Review, 54*, 413–435.

Sakamoto, M. (2000). *Raising bilingual and trilingual children: Japanese immigrant parents' child-rearing experiences*. Unpublished doctoral dissertation, Ontario Institute for Studies in Education/University of Toronto, Toronto, ON.

Sangwine, J. (1988). The ESL/D classroom as publishing house. *TESL Talk, 18*(1), 170–178.

Verplaetse, L.S. (1998). How content teachers interact with English language learners. *TESOL Journal, 7*(5), 24–28.

CHAPTER 6

Untangling Second Language Writers' and Teachers' Knots With Reformulation

SHARON LAPKIN

After more than three decades of research on the second language (L2) proficiency of French immersion students, the conventional wisdom is that, although these students understand spoken and written French very well, they have difficulty writing and speaking grammatically correct French. English as a second language (ESL) students in the United States are learning English in similar content-based classrooms through school subjects such as social studies or science. In the case of ESL students, teachers may notice that the ability to speak English develops quite quickly, perhaps within several months of arrival in the United States. Cummins (see Baker & Hornberger, 2001) has established that although children may develop a surface fluency in speaking English, they may take as long as five to seven years of schooling to reach native speaker levels, particularly in their use of English grammar, spelling, and vocabulary.

In Canadian immersion programs and U.S. ESL programs, teachers integrate content and language learning so language learning occurs "incidentally" as teachers and students move through the curriculum. Weaver (1996) states, "Substantive evidence suggests that basic grammatical competence is best developed through exposure to comprehensible input and through attempting to communicate in the target language relatively unhampered by initial concerns about correctness" (p. 55).

Weaver underlines the importance of reading to provide models of rich, correct target-language use. One way that I have found to provide target-language models that are meaningful for students is to reformulate the students' grammatically incorrect writing into writing that follows grammar conventions.

A colleague and I have experimented with a reformulation strategy for teaching writing in a French immersion context that holds promise for untangling L2 learning and teaching knots in ESL as well. The essence of untangling the knots lies in moving students beyond surface fluency to an accurate and rhetorically effective command of the written language.

Reformulation, Collaboration, and L2 Writing

Anyone who teaches writing in an L2 has probably spent some time reformulating students' texts. Reformulation involves the rewriting of an L2 (French, in the examples presented in this chapter) text by a highly proficient target-language speaker. Allwright, Woodley, and Allwright (1988) point out that reformulations usually differ in many ways from students' original texts because changes are made at all levels (lexical, grammatical, and discourse) of the text. Cohen (1989) distinguishes between text reconstruction (correcting grammatical and surface errors in a text) and reformulation, or rewriting the text stylistically so it reads as if a native speaker had written it. In the work my colleague and I have done (Swain & Lapkin, 1998), we combine the two stages and use the term *reformulation* to cover both. The reformulation makes the meaning clearer and also allows for the implicit correction of formal errors. When students compare their writing to a reformulated version, they notice how the grammar in their writing differs from that of conventional English writing. This noticing process may lead to learning, especially if these comparisons take place during collaborative activities with their peers.

Because most ESL students need help to compare their version with the reformulated text (Cohen, 1983), providing opportunities to talk through the differences is vital. In working their way through the text and noticing changes, students discuss why the changes might have been made. They confront their language problems and work together to resolve them; metaphorically speaking, they untangle the knots in their understanding of how the L2 works. Collaboration encourages students to talk in the target language and helps them recognize linguistic problems in their own writing. They can then solve the problems together, pooling the linguistic resources of the group. When they work collaboratively to solve language problems, students may notice and discuss new vocabulary and aspects of grammar and discourse (e.g., coherence) that might be left unnoticed if they work alone. The act of writing and the collaborative dialogues that ensue provide occasions for language learning (Swain & Lapkin, 1998) as students share the role of expert and get help from one another during their discussion about the reformulated text (Brooks & Swain, 2002).

Based on a sense of where the students are in their L2 development, teachers can provide targeted help, strategically tailored to students' needs. Mantello (1996, 2002) experiments with reformulation with adolescent students. Her French as a second language (FSL) students are in grade 8 in an extended French program, having recently begun their intensive exposure to French. Mantello reformulates students' texts, paying special attention to the compound past tense. What strikes her is the extent to which her students learn aspects of language beyond the target structure:

> The reformulation technique worked especially well with a strong student (Annie) who found it both challenging and stimulating. Not only did Annie's proficiency with the passé composé improve but so did her writing as a whole. For example, she began to pay close attention to her writing style, various organizational features, and basic mechanics. She [also] attempted to vary her sentence structure. (1996, p. 130)

Students in Mantello's classroom whose French skills were not as strong benefited more from focusing strictly on the target structure in their writing—that is, concentrating on one feature of the language at a time.

The information presented in this chapter relates to grade 7 students who have had much more exposure to French and have reached an intermediate level of proficiency. Our participants are young adolescents enrolled in an early immersion program who had begun the program in kindergarten. The entire curriculum is delivered in French in grades 1 and 2, and a period of English language arts is introduced in grade 3. By grade 5, the instructional day is divided evenly between subjects taught in English and French.

Learning in Progress: Two Examples

In an ongoing series of studies (see, for example, Swain & Lapkin, 2001), we are finding that presenting L2 students with reformulated texts and giving them the chance to discuss differences between their own writing and a target-language version are successful in moving them along in their L2 writing development. To maximize opportunities for such discussion, we developed two multistage tasks, the stages of which are summarized in Figure 6.1.

In Stage 1, writing, pairs of students either write a story based on a set of pictures (jigsaw task) or listen to a taped story, take notes, and reconstruct the story from their notes in a dictogloss task (Swain & Lapkin, 2001). The dictogloss (Wajnryb, 1990) consists of a text read aloud two

FIGURE 6.1 TASK STAGES				
Stage 1 Writing (Pretest)	Stage 2 Noticing	Stage 3 Stimulated Recall	Stage 4 Posttest	Stage 5 Interviews
30 minutes, in French	10 minutes, in French	40 minutes, in English	15 minutes for each student	15–20 minutes for each student

times at normal speaking speed. Students take notes as they listen to the text twice and then collaborate to reconstruct it. In Stage 2, noticing, students compare their text to a reformulation of it, highlighting changes that they notice between their original and the reformulated version. We show them a videotape of their noticing activity in Stage 3, stimulated recall, and ask them to reflect aloud on what they had noticed and why. Each student individually rewrites the original story in Stage 4, posttest. We then interview students in Stage 5 to debrief them about the tasks and their reactions to them.

Example 1: Nina and Dara

Nina and Dara, two seventh-grade French immersion students of average and above-average ability in French, respectively, have written a narrative collaboratively, based on a set of pictures. This example shows their dialogue as they consider a reformulated version of the last sentence of their story. That sentence has the protagonist of their story trying to catch up with (*rattraper* is the correct verb in French) her friend Mike so they can go to school together. The reformulator had changed their verb (*attraper*—to catch) to *rattraper*. Here is what they notice:

Nina: *d'attra...de rattrape...*   (to catch...to catch up...)

Dara: *de rattraper* (to catch up with...)

Nina: *de rattraper son ami Mike?* (to catch up with her friend Mike?)

(Please note that some theorists explicitly include vocabulary as part of grammatical competence [e.g., Harley, Allen, Cummins, & Swain, 1990]. Weaver [1996] contends that while "teaching the meaningful parts of words" does not neatly fall into the domain of grammar, it does "help readers learn to decipher words and expand their vocabularies by attending to the meaningful parts of words" [p. 187].)

Later, when the two students rewrite the original story (Stage 4, posttest), they both use the correct verb, *rattraper*. The noticing session allows them to arrive at the correct form. This new knowledge is consolidated in the next stage of the multistage task, namely, a stimulated recall session. In that session, we stop the videotape we had made of the noticing session and ask the students to reflect on what they had noticed. Their collaborative dialogue leads them to figure out what the previously unknown verb means. At this stage of the activity, we interact with the students, but it is Nina and Dara who do the work:

Nina:	I think ours is right because she is not like re-catching...
Dara:	Yeah, so...
Nina:	catching him again.... It's the first time...
Researcher:	So that's the difference for you between *attraper* and *rattraper*?
Dara:	Yeah, like *rattraper* it's like re-catch.
Nina:	Well, no...
Dara:	*Rattraper* it's like, yeah!
Nina:	Well, maybe *rattraper*.
Dara:	She's trying to catch him.
Nina:	Maybe, maybe *rattraper* means like she is trying to catch up to him...
Researcher:	Well, you got it.

Swain defines collaborative dialogue as "the joint construction of language—or knowledge about language—by two or more individuals...it's where language use and language learning can co-occur" (1997, p. 115; see also Swain, 2000). This is exactly what we see happening in the example: Through their dialogue, Nina and Dara figure out that the prefix *re* (or *r* before a vowel, as in *rattraper*), which usually means "again," changes the meaning of *attraper* to the idiomatic "catch up with," and both students then use the appropriate verb when they individually write the story again.

These two short excerpts constitute what we have called language-related episodes (LREs), defined as any part of the collaborative dialogue in which students talk about the language they are producing and then question or reflect on their language use, or correct themselves or others (e.g., Swain & Lapkin, 1998). Nina and Dara produce 21 LREs in the noticing session, noticing 21 of the 29 changes the reformulator had made to their text (most of the ones they fail to notice are French accents or punctuation marks such as commas). In the stimulated recall session, we count 23 LREs. In the posttest stories, each learner incorporates about 80% of the changes the reformulator had made, indicating that she has learned the grammatical, lexical, or discourse feature in question.

Example 2: Sam and Marnie

A second example comes from Sam and Marnie's work as they struggle to learn the form of a French pronominal verb. Sam is an above-average student who had also spent one year living in a French environment, and Marnie is an average student. In their story, based on a dictogloss, the main character is awakened by her alarm clock, does not want to get up, and lies down again or goes back to bed. The context requires the verb *se recoucher*, supplied by the reformulator. Like a subset of verbs in French, *se recoucher* occurs in the pronominal or reflexive form (Connors & Ouellette, 1996); an awkward literal translation of *elle se recouche* would be "she lies herself down again" or "she puts herself to bed." The idiomatic translation is "she lies down again" or "she goes back to bed." Sam and Marnie had written *elle retourne au lit*, literally, "she returns (goes back to) bed." This is a non–target-like structure.

Although this set of LREs (see dialogue below) focuses on formal properties of pronominal verbs in French, there remains a meaning component as Sam and Marnie discuss what a *verbe réfléchi* (pronominal verb) implies about meaning. In the noticing stage (Stage 2 in Figure 6.1, page 69), the students notice that the reformulator used the pronominal verb *se recoucher* to describe what the sleepy protagonist does (i.e., she goes back to bed) when the alarm clock so rudely awakens her. The following excerpt from the stimulated recall stage shows the researcher probing to find out if the students understand why the verb takes the pronominal form. Essentially, this is a discussion about transitivity, because the contrast is between *elle se recouche* (she goes back to bed) and *elle recouche le bébé* (she puts the baby to bed).

> A Researcher: Why would you use *se* there?
>
> Marnie: *Se* because it's like herself…. She like not to anybody else.

B	Sam:	*C'est un verbe réfléchi?* (It's a reflexive verb?)
	Marnie:	*réfléchi.*
	Researcher:	Is it possible to use this verb, uh, without *se*? Like, for example, *Elle recouche le bébé? Elle se recouche?* (She puts the baby to bed? She goes back to bed.)
	Sam:	Yes.
	Marnie:	Yeah, yeah.
C	Marnie:	Yes, yes, you could use it without *se* probably.
	Researcher:	Do you know of any other verbs that work like that? That could work with or without?
	Sam:	There are a lot of things here like *peigne les cheveux* (comb one's hair). *Se peigne* you could probably use *peigne les cheveux* to like to someone else 'cause...
	Marnie:	*Se brosse* (brush one's...) too.
	Sam:	Yeah...someone brushes another person's teeth.
	Marnie:	Yeah, like you are a baby or something. I don't know [laughter]. No, like seriously...
	Sam:	...or a dog or something [laughter].
	Marnie:	Yeah, and *s'habille* (to get dressed) I guess you can.... Yes, like if you dress a baby.

In *A* the research assistant asks, "Why would you use *se* there?" A sustained conversation ensues in which the students engage in metatalk (talk about language) centering on what constitutes a pronominal verb as they understand it. In this discussion, they are aided by the research assistant's questions. Marnie tries to state a principle ("It's like herself.... She like not to anybody else") underlying one subset of pronominal verbs; "The action of such verbs is reflected back onto the subject, their meaning remains the same when they are used in their non-pronominal form" (formally explained by Connors & Ouellette, 1996, p. 219). It seems clear that Marnie has understood the rule.

In *B* Sam asks, "C'est un verbe réfléchi?" and Marnie laughingly confirms that it is a pronominal verb. Then, the research assistant asks if the verb can be used in its non-pronominal form, providing contrasting examples (*Elle recouche le bébé/Elle se recouche*). Sam and Marnie both respond with a definitive "yes."

In *C*, Marnie seems to hesitate about whether *recoucher* can be used without *se*, and the researcher, seeking to elicit the general principle, asks whether there are any other verbs that function in a similar way. In the ensuing dialogue, Sam and Marnie together generate several verbs that do indeed work in the same way, among them *[se]peigner, [se]brosser, [s']habiller*.

In this set of LREs, the students notice the reformulator's change (to *se recouche*), offering no comment on the reflexive verb in Stage 2 and a correct explanation in Stage 3 (when prompted by the researcher). Sam and Marnie appear to learn the item *se recouche* (both students use it in Stage 4) and to consolidate their knowledge of a rule about a subset of pronominal verbs, those with a reflexive reading.

Sam and Marnie produce 9 LREs in Stage 2, noticing 9 of the 15 changes the reformulator made to their text. In Stage 3 (see *A*, *B*, and *C*), they generate 10 LREs. In their posttest stories, one student incorporates 13 and the other 14 of the 15 changes in the reformulation, indicating that considerable learning has occurred.

The Students' Knots: How Reformulation Facilitates Language Learning

From these examples, we conclude that the noticing that pairs of students do when they compare their own writing to that of an "expert," along with the sustained discussion of changes made to their story, creates opportunities for language learning. As Marnie told us in her interview,

> You get to see the corrections yourself and then know that [what you wrote is] wrong, instead of just someone just saying "oh no, that's not right." You get to think about if they are right or wrong if it is written beside you.

In our examples, students work together to solve some of the knots they must unravel to move forward in their L2 development. In order to accomplish this, even these relatively strong students require some assistance from a more competent target-language speaker. Nina and Dara get confirmation that their negotiated understanding of *rattraper* is correct. Sam and Marnie's interaction with the researcher undoubtedly consolidates their knowledge about intransitive pronominal verbs and their transitive counterparts. The researcher, then, plays a teacher-like role in the multistage task.

The Teachers' Knots: Ideas for Using Reformulation to Teach ESL Writing

Our research to date suggests that teachers can be confident that, even in their absence, students can engage in productive collaborative dialogue using one another and a reformulated text as resources. As students learn the target language together, Linda Schmeichel, a French immersion teacher, suggests that the key is for the teacher to model collaborative dialogue for the students before engaging them in these activities (personal communication, April 2002). This provides students with direction on how to participate effectively in the pair or group interactions.

It is undoubtedly difficult for teachers to set up multistage tasks for all their students simultaneously and monitor all the pairs as they work together. But teachers can select one story and its reformulation for whole-group discussion (see Thornbury, 1997) or participate in the task with one pair at a time. Still, as we have seen, at some point teacher intervention is crucial. Lest reformulating whole student texts appear overwhelming, teachers can choose short texts or parts of texts to reformulate.

If the pair or group discussions can be taped (perhaps one group on each occasion), teachers can listen to the tape at their leisure and discover which lexical items, grammatical structures, and so on constitute knots to be untangled. These can then form the basis of a minilesson (Weaver, 1996). Linda Schmeichel (personal communication, April 2002) offers two other possibilities:

1. Students listen to their own tapes and come up with areas of linguistic weakness. The teacher would still address these problematic areas, and the students would be even more engaged in linguistic analysis and perhaps take greater ownership over what they have learned in the reformulation activity.

2. Students keep a reformulation journal in which they note what kinds of things they noticed when they were comparing the two texts. Over the course of the week, the teacher can have short conferences with each pair of students and discuss their journal entries.

Because French immersion is a content-based program, teachers can use reformulation to integrate the teaching of language into content lessons. Kowal (1997), a grade 8 immersion teacher, uses a dictogloss with content from the environmental studies syllabus to focus on the teaching of the present tense in French. Although she does not reformulate student texts, she compares student-generated texts with the original (well-formed) dictogloss passage. She uses a whole-class approach, using two overheads, one with an anonymous student text chosen at random and the other with the original dictogloss.

Because writing is an integral part of the language arts and other components of the program, immersion teachers can integrate the reformulation strategy with writing that is a regular part of the curriculum. Further, they do not have to implement this type of activity on a weekly basis in order for it to be effective. Even a couple of times a term will prove effective. They can experiment with the strategy and modify its implementation according to their teaching context.

Conclusion

Reformulation is an effective approach to confronting the dilemma of how to provide increased opportunities for students to write in their target L2 and provide feedback to students in their zones of proximal development (Lantolf, 2000; Vygotsky, 1987). Building from the texts that students produce collaboratively, teachers identify and treat the language problems that are of immediate relevance to students—thus untangling several knots in the complex task of L2 teaching.

NOTE: The data referred to in this chapter were collected in the context of a grant from the Social Sciences and Humanities Research Council of Canada (#410-99-0269) to Merrill Swain and me. I would like to acknowledge with thanks valuable feedback I received on earlier drafts of this chapter from Gladys Jean, Shelley Peterson, Linda Schmeichel, Monika Smith, Merrill Swain, and Miles Turnbull.

REFERENCES

Allwright, R.L., Woodley, M.P., & Allwright, J.M. (1988). Investigating reformulation as a practical strategy for the teaching of academic writing. *Applied Linguistics, 9,* 236–256.

Baker, C., & Hornberger, N.H. (Eds.). (2001). *An introductory reader to the writings of Jim Cummins.* Clevedon, UK: Multilingual Matters.

Brooks, L., & Swain, M. (2002). *Collaborative writing and sources of feedback: How they support second language learning.* Toronto: Ontario Institute for Studies in Education/University of Toronto Modern Language Centre.

Cohen, A.D. (1983). Reformulating compositions. *TESOL Newsletter, 17*(6), 1–5.

Cohen, A.D. (1989). Reformulation: A technique for providing advanced feedback in writing. *Guidelines: A Periodical for Classroom Language Teachers, 11*(2), 1–9.

Connors, K., & Ouellette, B. (1996). Describing the meanings of French pronominal-verbal constructions for students of French-English translation. *Language Sciences, 18*(1/2), 213–226.

Harley, B., Allen, P., Cummins, J., & Swain, M. (1990). *The development of second language proficiency.* Cambridge, UK: Cambridge University Press.

Kowal, U.M. (1997). *French immersion students' language growth in French: Perceptions, patterns and programming.* Toronto: Ontario Institute for Studies in Education/University of Toronto.

Lantolf, J.P. (2000). Introducing sociocultural theory. In J.P. Lantolf (Ed.), *Sociocultural theory and second language learning* (pp. 1–26). Oxford, UK: Oxford University Press.

Mantello, M. (1996). *Selective error correction in intermediate extended French writing programs: A comparative study of reformulation and coded feedback.* Unpublished master's thesis, Ontario Institute for Studies in Education/University of Toronto, Toronto, ON.

Mantello, M. (2002). Error correction in the L2 classroom. In M. Turnbull, J.S. Bell, & S. Lapkin (Eds.), *From the classroom: Grounded activities for language learning* (pp. 134–138). Toronto: Canadian Modern Language Review.

Swain, M. (1997). Collaborative dialogue: Its contribution to second language learning. *Revista Canaria de Estudios Ingleses, 34,* 115–132.

Swain, M. (2000). The output hypothesis and beyond: Mediating acquisition through collaborative dialogue. In J.P. Lantolf (Ed.), *Sociocultural theory and second language learning* (pp. 97–114). Oxford, UK: Oxford University Press.

Swain, M., & Lapkin, S. (1998). Interaction and second language learning: Two adolescent French immersion students working together. *Modern Language Journal, 83,* 320–337.

Swain, M., & Lapkin, S. (2001). Focus on form through collaborative dialogue: Exploring task effects. In M. Bygate, P. Skehan, & M. Swain (Eds.), *Researching pedagogic tasks: Second language learning, teaching, and testing* (pp. 99–118). Harlow, Essex, UK: Pearson.

Thornbury, S. (1997). Reformulation and reconstruction: Tasks that promote "noticing." *ELT Journal, 51,* 326–335.

Vygotsky, L.S. (1987). *The collected works of L.S. Vygotsky. Volume 1. Thinking and speaking.* New York: Plenum.

Wajnryb, R. (1990). *Grammar dictation.* Oxford, UK: Oxford University Press.

Weaver, C. (1996). *Teaching grammar in context.* Portsmouth, NH: Heinemann.

CHAPTER 7

A Tightly Tangled Knot: The Influence of Teachers' Gender Perceptions on Their Assessment of Student Writing

SHELLEY PETERSON

If you were asked to describe girls' writing and boys' writing, would you say that girls' stories are generally about female characters who develop caring relationships with others in order to solve problems? Would you also say that boys tend to write more violent stories about male characters who overcome obstacles through high-intensity, dangerous actions? If so, you would be in agreement with a number of researchers (Gray-Schlegel & Gray-Schlegel, 1995–1996; Romatowski & Trepanier-Street, 1987; Tuck, Bayliss, & Bell, 1985) who have examined gender characteristics of students' writing.

You would also be in agreement with the teachers I surveyed in my research (Peterson, 1998, 2001). When I asked grade 3 and 6 teachers in Alberta and Ohio, where I lived and worked before moving to Ontario, to identify the writers of narrative and persuasive papers as girls or boys (if they felt that they could) and to identify the gender characteristics (gender markers) within the papers, teachers generally said that girls and boys in elementary classrooms choose stereotypical topics, characters, and conflict resolution methods when they write fiction. These are not the only gender differences that teachers noted. Teachers also referred to girls' and boys' competence as writers when describing gender characteristics of the narrative and persuasive writing. They talked about girls' writing as being better organized, more descriptive, having better developed plots, and showing a more sophisticated use of writing conventions and sentence structures. In interviews in which I asked teachers to describe gender differences that they had observed in their students' classroom writing, they identified girls as better writers than boys, as a general rule.

In this chapter, I highlight two knots in writing assessment—the different expectations that the teachers in my studies held for girls' and boys'

77

writing and the problems that these expectations could create in a climate that encourages objectivity in writing assessment. Then I present suggestions based on my experience in working with teachers and students for addressing the influence of gender perceptions on writing assessment.

Knots in Writing Assessment: Teachers' Gender Expectations

Gender Stereotypes

Most teachers participating in my studies (Peterson, 1998, 2001) felt they were able to identify a writer's gender based on characteristics such as the protagonist's gender and the other qualities I have described. They identified the gender of the writer without having the writer's name on the paper. With few exceptions, teachers characterized girls as being more competent narrative writers than boys. They described papers whose writers they perceived to be girls as interesting, complete, and "showing a lot of thought." Teachers felt that girls used more sophisticated vocabulary than boys, as well.

When the teachers in my research studies described the writer's competence, they had different perceptions depending on whether they thought the writer of a narrative or persuasive paper was a boy or a girl. In one narrative, for example, two female grade 6 teachers who thought the writer was a girl found evidence of "good spelling" and "details," whereas a female teacher who thought the writer was a boy felt that there was a "lack of description" and "short sentences." Another female teacher found the ending weak, explaining that "boys have more problems with conclusions." Repeatedly, teachers talked about the strengths of the writing when they thought the writer was a girl, and they talked about the weaknesses of the writing when they thought the writer was a boy. For example, one female grade 6 teacher—when referring to a short persuasive paper that contained many convention errors—said, "Most students who write so poorly are boys."

When the teachers in my research studies talked about gender differences that they had observed in the writing of their students, they explained that elementary school girls were more emotionally and intellectually mature than boys their age. This maturity, they felt, gave girls a stronger base for learning to write. Teachers said that girls were more conscientious and that they were more self-confident as writers. Teachers used words such as "careful" and "hardworking" to describe girls as writers. They described boys as "careless writers" and said that boys "want to finish quickly."

This trend toward perceiving girls as better writers than boys certainly matched the trend in scores on large-scale writing assessments. For as long as the large-scale tests of writing have been administered, girls outperformed boys at all grades that were tested (grades 3, 4, 6, 8, and 9) on statewide, provincewide, and national tests of writing competence in the United States, Canada, and the United Kingdom (Alberta Education, 1995; Applebee, Langer, & Mullis, 1986; Ohio Department of Education, 2000; Stobart, Elwood, & Quinlan, 1992). The gap widened in the higher grades. Indeed, recent reports of the Educational Testing Service show that the gap in writing between boys and girls at the eighth-grade level is over six times greater than the gender differences in mathematical reasoning (Cole, 1997). The disparity between boys' and girls' writing competence is clearly a knot that needs to be untangled.

This is particularly true when considering the results of a research study in Nigeria that showed a correlation between teachers' expectations and girls' and boys' literacy performance. When Johnson (1973–1974) asked Nigerian teachers about their expectations for girls and boys as readers and writers, teachers expected boys to be better writers than girls. Their expectations were met on large-scale assessments, as boys did perform better than their female peers. The researchers concluded that what teachers expected was often what they ended up seeing in their students' writing. The reverse was true in Alberta and Ohio. Teachers perceived girls to be better writers, a perception that was borne out in the provincewide and statewide writing evaluations.

As demonstrated in the interviews with teachers in my research studies, one of the assumptions that guided writing assessment contributed to the very problem it was designed to avoid, that of inequitable assessment. In the next section of this chapter, I discuss—as another knot in the gender and assessment tangle—the assumption that objectivity is necessary for unbiased assessment.

An Emphasis on Objectivity

Within a climate of standardization and reliability in writing assessment, teachers have been encouraged to use three direct assessment tools: analytic rubrics, holistic scoring, and primary trait scoring (Dahl & Farnan,

1998). Analytic rubrics address each of a number of components of writing (e.g., ideas, organization, use of language, and use of grammar and writing conventions). Holistic scoring guides provide criteria for making overall judgments of the quality of a piece of writing. Primary trait scoring focuses on one aspect of the writing that defines the major purpose achieved using a particular form of writing. For example, in a narrative paper, the writer's use of a narrative structure (the organization of events into an introduction, a development of a problem, and a resolution of a problem) might be the primary trait on which the paper is assessed.

Using an analytic rubric based loosely on the criteria within a rubric developed by the Ohio Department of Education (1999), the following narrative, written by a sixth-grade boy, might be evaluated in this way. (I highlight this rubric because it was used by teachers in my Ohio study.)

> Once, long ago there was a legend of a mystical power that was responsible for all the major changes around the world. The power could fall into anyones hands good or evil. When it changed hands it would never be given to someone else until the former one that had it, had past away. Whenever someone received the power they would never let anyone know, for fear they would do something to them.
>
> One year after a great battle between to mighty nations the power fell into the possession of a magician named Merlin. While in his possession he contained the power into a wand making it easier to control. This Magic wand was responsible for the rise and fall of every great nation. To this day no one knows who has the wand.
>
> **Present Time**
>
> As doctor Brenda Montoya was giving her lesson on heart surgery her mind drifted away from her to a distant place. All her life, Emelia Earhart had been Dr. Montoyas's inspiration. She longed to be in a plane clutching the control stick guiding the plane. But she came out of her day dream stumbling her words.
>
> After finishing her lecture Brenda leaves the class room coming out on the street. As she reached her car a strange man bumped into her then to the ground gasping for a breath. But whatever he meant to tell Brenda was never said. For he was at an age of 500 and it was his time. But what Brenda didn't know was that he stuffed something in her purse.
>
> After Brenda had gotten home, she noticed her purse was glowing "How strange" she said. When she opened her purse and saw the sparkling wand she knew what it was. She had heard the story of it many times. She fell to her knees crying.

After she had stopped crying, she thought to herself, "Now I have the power to do anything", At first she was scared, but then she remembered the saying that fueled her inspiration." Then she closed her eyes and wished to fly.

When she opened her eyes she was in the seat of a huge rocket ship, cutting through the sky like it was nothing. Only to disappear in the bright blue sky, never to be seen again.

Using the Ohio scale of 1 to 4, with level 3 representing the expectations for the grade level, this paper might be scored at 3 in the ideas category because it has ample supporting details and has a clear focus—the influence of the magic wand on its bearer. The writer demonstrates a higher than grade level of sophistication in trying to tie two contexts and time periods together. This task is fairly well achieved, although the writer could include more information about Merlin's choice of Brenda as the bearer of the wand and information about what happened to the wand when Brenda disappeared. In the organization category, the paper might be scored at level 3 because the events are presented in a logical order with an apparent beginning, middle, and end. Each section needs to be further developed, however, with clearer links between sections. In the use of language category, a score of 4 might be assigned because there are numerous examples of specific words and phrases (e.g., "longed to be in a plane clutching the control stick" and "fueled her inspiration"). In addition, the writer uses sophisticated sentence structures with numerous complex sentences containing dependent and independent clauses (e.g., "After finishing her lecture Brenda leaves the class room coming out on the street."). In the use of grammar and writing conventions category, a score of 3 might be assigned because the paper has occasional grammar and spelling and punctuation errors that do not interfere with the message. For the most part, the grammar and punctuation errors are a result of taking risks in using more sophisticated sentence structures.

Using the holistic rubric developed by the Ohio Department of Education (1999), the paper might be scored at a level 3 (the score assigned most often by teachers in my research study). Although one of the criteria, use of language, actually fits within level 4, a holistic score of 3 is assigned because most elements of the writing fall within the level 3 descriptors. Primary trait evaluation would likely result in a score of 3, as well, because the narrative structure is deemed to be characteristic of level 3 (i.e., has a logical order with an apparent beginning, middle, and end, although some lapses may occur).

When teachers use rubrics such as those described earlier, they are expected to assess students' writing objectively, focusing on the scoring criteria and pushing aside their background knowledge, experiences, values, emotions, and motivations. Given currently recognized perspectives on reading (Goodman, 1970; Rosenblatt, 1978), however, we know it is impossible to read any text objectively. Each time a reader reads a piece of writing, the reader's perceptions, thoughts, and values interact with the meanings embedded within the writing to create a new set of meanings and impressions. Assessing writing is certainly a subjective endeavor.

The subjective nature of assessing student writing was reinforced in the inconsistencies in the scores that the grades 3 and 6 teachers in the Ohio study assigned to the narrative and persuasive papers I sent to them. The scores for one persuasive paper at both grade levels ranged from 1 to 4 (below grade level to exceeding grade-level expectations). Teachers assigned scores ranging either from 2 to 4 or from 1 to 3 to all the other papers. The range of scores assigned to papers in the Alberta study was within two scoring levels on the five-level analytic scoring guide used by the Alberta Ministry of Education, as well. In this study, there were no papers for which teachers' scores ranged from below grade-level expectations to exceeding grade-level expectations, however.

The range of scores that teachers in the two studies assigned to student writing underscores the impossibility of universal readings of a piece of writing, an understanding that is well supported within research on writing evaluation (Barritt, Stock, & Clark, 1986; Purves, 1992). Yet, the perception of objectivity in writing assessment persists, as demonstrated by teachers in my Ohio and Alberta studies.

In interviews, teachers in my studies emphasized repeatedly how important and yet how difficult it was for them to be fair and objective in their assessments of student writing. They dismissed the possibility that bias toward one gender or the other could play a role in their evaluations of student writing. Indeed, teachers asserted, "I don't think about gender. I just try to look at the writing." More than two thirds of teachers in the Ohio study and 40% of teachers in the Alberta study actively avoided considering social and cultural influences in their assessments of students' writing. Comments such as, "I'm just keying in on the [criteria] of the scoring guide so much that gender is the furthest thing from my mind" were common in both studies. Teachers placed great faith in the rubrics as objective representations of global standards that did not favor girls over boys.

I would never argue against the importance of fairness and equity in writing assessment. Indeed, the research I have read on writing assessment emphasizes the importance of fairness as strongly as the teachers in my two research studies do (Huot, 1990). Clearly, striving for fairness in writing assessment is not the problem. Rather, it is the blind faith in the use of rubrics as filters for any gender assumptions that teachers might have that presents a problem. (Teachers communicated these assumptions very clearly when they identified gender markers in the writing and talked about boys' and girls' classroom writing.) This faith creates a false sense of having done everything possible to achieve fairness. An example from my Alberta study illustrates the influence of teachers' gender perceptions on their assessment of student writing, even while using supposedly objective analytic rubrics.

Teachers in the Alberta study assigned grades to the papers in addition to identifying each writer's gender. When I compared the scores that were assigned to one of five papers that teachers felt were written by boys with those of papers that teachers felt were written by girls, I found a favoring of girls over boys in the marking of one paper. This paper was written by a girl whose gender was either incorrectly identified or unidentifiable to 77% of participating teachers. Teachers who identified the writer of the paper as a boy assigned significantly lower scores than did teachers who identified the writer as a girl. Yet, at the same time that teachers were scoring the paper significantly lower if they thought the writer was a boy, they were also asserting that their scoring was objective. They insisted that the writer's perceived gender had no influence on their evaluation of the writing. These are the tensions that require further examination and thought.

In summary, two knots that contribute to disparities in the assessment of boys' and girls' writing are teachers' perceptions of girls as better writers than boys and the assumptions underlying current writing assessment practices: that the use of rubrics can wash out the effects of teachers' gender perceptions and result in an objective and fair assessment. In the next section, I direct suggestions to classroom teachers for untangling these knots in their assessment of classroom writing and in their participation in the marking of large-scale writing assessments within their schools and school districts.

Untangling the Knots in Writing Assessment

To begin untangling the gender and assessment knot, teachers need to examine their own beliefs, expectations, values, feelings, and experiences regarding gender in student writing. Teachers in my preservice and graduate classes and I consider questions such as the following: What gender patterns have teachers observed in their own and in their students' writing over the years? How do girls and boys talk about their own writing in student-teacher conferences? Are there gender patterns in the comments that teachers write on student papers and provide during student-teacher conferences and author groups? What aspects (ideas, organization, use of language, use of grammar, and writing conventions) do teachers emphasize when evaluating student writing, and are there gender patterns in terms of who experiences the greatest success within each area?

Asking these questions in conversations with other teachers is valuable, particularly if teachers within a school, school district, or group of markers of large-scale writing examinations wish to base their scoring of student writing on shared perceptions of gender in student writing. In addition, if fairness in large-scale writing assessments is to be achieved, examiners must recognize the subjective nature of reading and assessing student writing. Having at least two readers for every piece of writing is critical in order to give a more complete picture of each student's competence as a writer.

Teachers' awareness of the ways in which a definition of writing that meets or exceeds the grade-level expectations matches teachers' expectations for girls' writing is a first step toward reducing the possibility of gender-biased marking. In my teacher education classes, teachers and I look at the assessment criteria, thinking about ways to emphasize elements that teachers identify as strengths in their boys' classroom writing, such as the writer's craft in creating suspense and in taking characters through action-filled, plot-driven stories. We modify the provincial rubric to accommodate these additional criteria. The new criteria also become part of the discussion when students give feedback to one another on their writing in author groups, in students' self-assessment, and in student-teacher conferences.

These assessment criteria are as follows: (1) the unique twists on familiar gender meanings that they express in their writing, (2) the parts of their writing that they feel express their personality and who they are as girls or boys, (3) the parts that give students the greatest pleasure to create, (4) the parts that reflect a new discovery about themselves as boys or girls within their social world, and (5) the parts that reflect their experimentation with new ideas.

Teachers also highlight the additional criteria in student-teacher conferences. For example, a student-teacher conference with the grade 6 boy who wrote the narrative about Brenda Montoya includes a discussion of the ways in which he uses his background experience with narratives that bring readers through various times and contexts to create a unique and appealing plot. The boy's teacher recognizes that he tried something new in using a female character in his story. She asks him about his rationale for doing so and how it feels for a boy to write about a girl. To provide for a richer experience of experimenting with alternative gender roles, she encourages the boy to consult some girls in the class about questions such as, How could the boy change his narrative to show a better understanding of what the female character might be thinking and doing? The teacher considers these questions to be part of an author's research process, as the boy gathers information to develop his characters. In addition, the teacher talks with students about appropriate responses to each other's writing when listening to the polished writing of peers who take a risk and decide to cross gender lines in their writing. She reads aloud books written by male authors about typically feminine topics and female characters, as well as books written by female authors about male characters and typically masculine topics, as models of writers who cross gender lines.

As I describe examples of what my students and I have been attempting in order to address the knot of gender disparities in the assessment of student writing, I am not saying that these practices are the only ways to address the issue. They are my initial, tentative steps toward addressing what I see as something too important for us to continue to overlook in our teaching. My biggest hope is that this chapter presents a provocative perspective on the issue because this is one knot in teaching writing that we have only begun to untangle.

NOTE: The research described in this chapter was funded by an Elva Knight Research Grant from the International Reading Association. I appreciate the Association's support of my research.

REFERENCES

Alberta Education. (1995). *Achievement testing program provincial report*. Edmonton, AB: Author.

Applebee, A.N., Langer, J.A., & Mullis, I.V. (1986). *The writing report card: Writing achievement in American schools* (Report No. 15-W-02). Princeton, NJ: Educational Testing Service.

Barritt, L., Stock, P.L., & Clark, F. (1986). Researching practice: Evaluating assessment essays. *College Composition and Communication, 37*(3), 315–325.

Cole, N. (1997). *The ETS gender study: How females and males perform in educational settings.* Princeton, NJ: Educational Testing Service.

Dahl, K.L., & Farnan, N. (1998). *Children's writing: Perspectives from research.* Newark, DE: International Reading Association; Chicago: National Reading Conference.

Goodman, K. (1970). Behind the eye: What happens in reading? In K.S. Goodman & O. Niles (Eds.), *Reading: Process and program* (pp. 3–38). Urbana, IL: National Council of Teachers of English.

Gray-Schlegel, M., & Gray-Schlegel, T. (1995–1996). An investigation of gender stereotypes as revealed through children's creative writing. *Reading Research and Instruction, 35*(2), 160–170.

Huot, B. (1990). The literature of direct writing assessment: Major concerns and prevailing trends. *Review of Educational Research, 60*(2), 237–263.

Johnson, D.D. (1973–1974). Sex differences in reading across cultures. *Reading Research Quarterly, 9,* 67–85.

Ohio Department of Education (1999). *Scoring guide: Writing.* Columbus, OH: Author. Retrieved from http://www.ode.state.oh.us/proficiency/sample_tests/sixth-6ptman02.pdf

Ohio Department of Education. (2000). *Ohio sixth-grade proficiency test results: Gender and ethnic March 2000 test administration.* Columbus, OH: Author.

Peterson, S. (1998). Evaluation and teachers' perceptions of gender in sixth-grade student writing. *Research in the Teaching of English, 33*(2), 181–208.

Peterson, S. (2001). Teachers' assessment of girls' and boys' narrative and persuasive writing. In J.V. Hoffman, D.L. Shallert, C.M. Fairbanks, J. Worthy, & B. Maloch (Eds.), *50th yearbook of the National Reading Conference* (pp. 483–494). Chicago: National Reading Conference.

Purves, A. (1992). Reflections on research and assessment in written composition. *Research in the Teaching of English, 26*(1), 108–122.

Romatowski, J.A., & Trepanier-Street, M.L. (1987). Gender perceptions: An analysis of children's creative writing. *Contemporary Education, 59*(1), 17–19.

Rosenblatt, L. (1978). *The reader, the text, the poem: The transactional theory of the literary work.* Carbondale, IL: Southern Illinois University Press.

Stobart, G., Elwood, J., & Quinlan, M. (1992). Gender bias in examinations: How equal are the opportunities? *British Educational Research Journal, 18*(3), 261–276.

Tuck, D., Bayliss, V., & Bell, M. (1985). Analysis of sex stereotyping in characters created by young authors. *Journal of Educational Research, 78*(4), 248–252.

Teaching Writing Using Multimedia and the Arts

THIS SECTION EXTENDS discussions of writing instruction to issues that would not have been commonplace to those who wrote the foundational works on teaching writing but that are becoming increasingly important to teachers in today's classrooms.

In chapter 8, Joseph Allin describes how an eighth-grade teacher paired his students with high school students who served as online mentors. He examines knots in using technology to teach writing, in particular, the lack of face-to-face dialogue when students receive feedback to their writing online.

In chapter 9, Carl Leggo addresses the neglect of poetry in elementary and middle-grade classrooms by identifying misconceptions about poetry and providing teaching suggestions that champion poetry writing as a creative endeavor that is accessible to all students. Cautioning against using formulas in teaching poetry writing, Carl explains how poetry writing can nurture writers who delight in the wonder of words.

In chapter 10, David Booth argues that drama provides personally significant contexts for students' writing and addresses knots posed by reluctant writers and writers who have difficulty going beyond superficial treatments of topics. Through linking drama and writing, students gain new perspectives that enrich their writing. In turn, the writing enhances the learning and interactions within the drama experiences.

In chapter 11, Jill Kedersha McClay tackles two knots—motivating the reluctant, resistant writer and integrating technology in sensible ways into writing instruction. Observing that many reluctant writers are looking for new challenges, she proposes that teachers and students push boundaries by taking up newer topics, forms, and media that are part of adolescents' everyday lives.

CHAPTER 8

Untying the Knot of Time Constraints: Using Technology to Extend Student Writing Beyond the Classroom

JOSEPH ALLIN

T ony, an eighth-grade classroom teacher, has long been committed to writers' workshop (Calkins, 1994; Graves, 1994), an instructional approach that engages students with their teacher and with each other in a complex, interactive process of producing publishable written compositions. However, finding adequate time for essential elements of writing workshop, such as drafting, revising, or conferencing, was problematic for Tony. Given the abundance of prescribed expectations for student writing outlined in the mandated curriculum, Tony was looking for an effective strategy to escape the knot of time constraints imposed by the curriculum and the structure of the school day. Much of the writing that students completed during Tony's class was narrative. Although his students were enthusiastic and confident narrative writers, Tony worried that not enough attention was being devoted to different types of writing. He wanted to find a way to encourage student writing for varied purposes and audiences.

Tony is not alone. The literature on process writing is filled with accounts of teachers expressing concern that time constraints caused by school structures form tight knots that limit student creativity and achievement. Beyond finding adequate blocks of time for students to write (Sudol & Sudol, 1991), teachers are concerned about finding time for student-teacher and peer conferences to provide students with feedback on their in-process writing (Biffignani, 1995; Westervelt, 1998). Teachers also express a need to have students bring their work to conclusion within some kind of time frame (Biffignani, 1995; Sudol & Sudol, 1991). Given the limited class time available, teachers are always anxious that it be used productively.

A progressive and innovative teacher, Tony devised a way to extend the writing workshop beyond the time and space of his eighth-grade classroom by using the Internet as a means of connectivity. In this chapter, I tell Tony's story with the hope that his innovative methodology may spur others to explore the potential of electronic learning forums made possible by the Internet as a means to enhance students' writing experience.

Extending the Instructional Day Electronically

Tony believed that the mentorship of a skillful writer would further his students' writing skills. He did not feel that it was necessary that this writing be completed under his direct tutelage in the classroom, however. He wondered whether the freedom to create text anywhere and at any time might serve as a stimulant to even more creative work by his students.

Tony saw electronic networking as a means to extend his classroom. He had read about the successes of other connected learning communities. For example, ORILLAS, a project designed by partner teachers, successfully supported student and teacher collaborations between classrooms in the United States, Puerto Rico, Argentina, Canada, and Mexico (Sayers, 1991). The Kids From Kanata project connected the children of the First Nations, Canada's aboriginal people, in classrooms across the country (Ord, 1998). In Project Headlight, conducted at Boston's Hennigan School, older students acting as technical consultants mentored younger schoolmates through online collaboration (Burnett, 1995). Writers in Electronic Residence (WIER) really sparked Tony's thinking. This project electronically connects students across Canada with writers who are all well-known Canadian authors. These authors read and consider the students' work, offer reactions and ideas, and guide discussions among the students. (See http://www.edu.yorku.ca/~wier/wierintro.html.) Using the capacity of electronic networking, WIER connects students across Canada with writers, teachers, and one another in an animated exchange of original writing and commentary. Drawing from the success of WIER and the other projects, Tony saw great potential in the collaborative power of connected learning communities. Computers were available in his classroom, the school library, and the local public library, all networked and interconnected by the Internet. Many of the students had computers and Internet access at home. Knowing this, Tony believed that students would be able to share their writing online.

Tony contacted the neighboring high school to seek out senior English students who were accomplished writers and might be willing to serve as online writing mentors. Six secondary students, each endorsed by their English teacher, volunteered to support the project. For their efforts, these students were promised credit toward required community work experience. Each high school student participated in a 90-minute workshop designed to address technical and logistical requirements as well as to explain the application of a rubric developed by Tony and his students. Tony's students used this rubric to guide their self-evaluation of expressive writing in the narrative form.

Using the word processor and student e-mail accounts provided by Microsoft Hotmail, students wrote and shared their work with members of the writing support group. These e-mail accounts were accessible from any computer having Internet access. In addition, students submitted final drafts of their writing to a classroom e-mail account from which the work would be forwarded to one of the secondary students serving as a writing mentor. Feedback and suggestions offered by the student mentor were directed by e-mail through the teacher back to the author. Three networked computers were located in the classroom. When a student was waiting to use a computer, a maximum of half an hour was allotted per use. With 30 students in the class, this provided at least half an hour per day for each student. The computers were in constant use.

With less class time being devoted to expressive writing, Tony saw additional classroom time becoming available to address argumentative and expository writing. He felt that class time would be better spent examining and producing different forms of writing intended to present opposing views or meant to explain, persuade, or inform. Although he valued the importance of his students writing expressive narrative, Tony anticipated that this work could be improved through a more independent effort by the student authors and with the support of the online writing mentors.

Classroom Dynamics

Instruction in Tony's classroom was organized around class and student projects, with an emphasis being placed on the interrelated nature of all learning. Tony emphasized reading and writing across the curriculum. Although whole-group instruction was offered, such sessions were brief. Students spent the bulk of their time engaged in individual and group activity. Groupings were formed on the basis of both achievement levels and interest. For much of the day, the children sat in groupings of five or six at work centers formed by two trapezoidal tables. During activity periods, the teacher's time was divided—sometimes offering small-group instruction, and otherwise circulating about the room to assist individuals.

The students used writing journals for a variety of purposes. These journals included personal reflections on favorite parts of stories that had been shared in class, story grammars (Dewsbury, 1994) detailing the components of forming a story, point form recollections about significant events and people, and notes from minilessons that Tony had taught. Students also maintained writing portfolios. The portfolio was organized in three sections: The first section included rough outlines and drafts of student writing; the middle section contained selected work that the students intended to finish after consultation with a writing partner; and the third section contained finished work that had been submitted for teacher evaluation. Written teacher comments in both the writing journal and the writing portfolio reflected the emphasis that was placed on the maintenance of these documents. The students were very aware that both editing and revision were integral parts of a recursive writing process designed to produce a logical, meaningful, detailed, and engaging written product.

Tony expected his students to be independent and self-directed learners. They maintained work logs in which they described learning outcomes to be achieved, defined related and specific tasks to be accomplished each day, and noted progress toward these intended outcomes. Tony also emphasized student self-evaluation. Often, the students assessed their work using rubrics that described levels of performance, and they included this self-assessment with the submission of a completed assignment. These rubrics were typically developed cooperatively with the class. Students frequently assisted one another, particularly at the computer center where two chairs sat in front of each computer. During the writing time, students formed writing support groups of three or four students who shared their work and offered constructive suggestions. Tony also used this time to join writing support groups and model appropriate questions and comments for the students similar to those in the author groups described by Bruce in chapter 3 in this book.

Although the students continued to produce high-quality writing in class, their online writing did not proceed as Tony had anticipated. It did not take Tony long to recognize that his attempt to escape the restraints of one knot appeared to have created a new bind. How could he live with the restriction on the students' use of class time for composing expressive narrative knowing that the quality of this writing produced outside of class was inferior? Tony asked his students for feedback to determine how he might strengthen his effort to extend the school day using the power of technology.

Lessons Learned From Tony's Experience

Tony's students told him that the use of technology did not allow them to work through the formulation of new ideas. They did not appreciate sharing their thoughts with strangers. Many of the students expressed difficulty relating to the secondary students who were serving as writing mentors. One of Tony's students expressed his concerns:

> Who are these geeks from the high school? We have never met them. So they read our work and cut it up. I don't think so. I know that they don't know our names, but I don't like this deal. All I can say is that I hope they fix my work up good before Mr. L. reads it.

Tony discovered that his students were unable to relate to the online writing mentors, who had no identity in the students' minds. Consequently, the students were reluctant to share their inner thoughts reflected in draft writing with the high school students.

The students also felt that writing at home for an online mentor audience made writing a much more isolated task and placed an emphasis on productivity rather than good writing processes. They lamented the loss of time devoted to student conferencing. They valued the in-class dialogue with peers and with Tony as helpful in clarifying ideas and stimulating new directions. With so much writing occurring outside the classroom, Tony also found that he lost access to information about his students' writing and learning because he was not able to observe his students at work. Furthermore, some of the students felt that the isolation of working at home offered an opportunity to avoid responsibility. In the words of one student,

> I don't know whether Mr. L. knows it but there are lots of web sites where you can get great stories. Lots of kids know about these sites. If you don't believe me, just check out The Evil House of Cheat (see http://www. cheathouse.com/uk/index.html) or School Sucks (see http://www.school sucks.com).

Given that Tony allowed his students to select many of their writing topics, the opportunity to submit others' work from the Internet was enhanced. Students hinted that peers who believed that value was placed only on the final written product may have found the Internet to be a source of writing to be handed in for a grade.

Tony realized that the success of his writing program hinged on his capacity to cultivate a cooperative learning community. Given the very personal nature of writing, it was essential that a mutual bond of trust existed between the students and their teacher. In this climate of trust, students felt assured that their most personal thoughts and ideas would be respected. This allowed them to overcome any sense of vulnerability associated with sharing a work in process. The restriction on the kinds of writing that would be entertained during class time and the expectation that students would share their most personal work with virtual strangers had created a new knot. In the absence of the spirit that formed a cooperative learning community, Tony recognized that his influence on the students' writing development was limited.

Future Use of Online Mentors

Some might suggest that Tony's experience adds credence to Birkerts's argument that "writing on the computer promotes process over product and favours the whole over the execution of the part" (1994, p. 158). Birkerts was concerned that students using the word processor would become caught up with the manipulation of text, rather than with the precise expression of deep personal thought. Certainly, Tony's students expressed an awareness of the capacity to import text and manipulate others' ideas when connected to the Internet. However, the students also felt that Tony did not value their writing as much as he had when he was providing more feedback on their writing.

Tony's experience reminds us of the importance of authenticity in any writing experience. Writing simply for a grade does not inspire a student's imagination or creativity. Thoughtful writing is created for a real audience. Although it is evident from Tony's experience that the computer can accommodate very poor writing processes, it can just as readily facilitate the very best writing practice. Surely, the writer's motivation dictates the thoughtfulness of the writing experience much more than the writing tool being used.

While recognizing the potential of the computer to bring writers together and facilitate such options as joint authorship, Smith (1983) cautions teachers to be cognizant of the complexity of children's language development. Tony's experience serves as a reminder that interactions among real people must always be primary in the assessment of any instructional methodology. With this thought foremost in his mind, Tony remains hopeful that his writing program can be extended using electronic means. He contemplates making several modifications, as identified in the following paragraphs.

1. Drawing from the model of WIER, Tony initially thought that he could use electronic connectivity to extend the support available to his student writers. His effort to provide anonymity for the students in sharing their work proved counterproductive, however. The students expressed a need to know and to trust those with whom they share draft writing. To gain acceptance, the student mentors must make themselves known to the students. Before interacting online, the writing mentors need to visit the classroom, share some of their own writing achievement, and join in the classroom discussion about writing issues.

The difference between Tony's program and WIER is that the professional writers whose advice is sought through WIER are not unknowns. They make themselves known and loved through their published work. In contrast, the high school students who worked with Tony's students were not familiar. Tony now believes that once his students have established a working relationship with the student mentors from the neighboring secondary school, they will willingly share their writing, enhancing new learning opportunities.

2. Rather than controlling the sharing of draft writing, Tony will encourage his students to share draft writing directly with one another and with the writing mentors via the Internet. With this free exchange among trusted individuals, the writing process will be enhanced. The Internet provides a means to connect Tony's students to the learning community beyond the school. By creating a place for students, their writing mentors, and their teacher to chat, Tony will extend the dialogue of the classroom.

3. Tony intends to provide a balance in the classroom time devoted to different forms of writing. He will continue to attend to those writing forms more relevant to the world of work and education: comparisons, business letters, précis, and public speeches. However, Tony wants to nurture his students' enthusiasm for writing workshops by providing adequate class time to engage in expressive narrative writing, as well.

Conclusion

As I reflect on Tony's experience, I am concerned about the sanctity of the teacher-student relationship. In today's school climate, bound by rigid structures and with its emphasis on accountability, is there the potential to force the effective teacher to abandon sound instructional practice in pursuit of higher levels of student achievement? New technologies offer teachers and students new opportunities, but they can never substitute for the benefits accrued from strong human relationships. The computer and the added connectivity it offers may well support students' learning by enhancing their capacity to communicate, but it will never be a substitute for the need for direct human exchange in the processes of teaching and learning. Learning to write takes time. Good writing is the product of much practice guided by trusted mentors.

REFERENCES

Biffignani, S. (1995). *I'm bored, I don't have anything to write about!* (Report No. CS-217216). East Lansing, MI: National Center for Research on Teacher Learning. (ERIC Document Reproduction Service No. ED444166)

Birkerts, S. (1994). *The Gutenberg elegies: The fate of reading in an electronic age.* Boston: Faber and Faber.

Burnett, G. (1995). Technology as a tool for urban classrooms. *ERIC Digest.* Retrieved from http://eric-web.tc.columbia.edu/digests/dig95.html

Calkins, L.M. (1994). *The art of teaching writing* (2nd ed.). Portsmouth, NH: Heinemann.

Dewsbury, A. (1994). *First steps: Writing resource book.* Portsmouth, NH: Heinemann.

Graves, D.H. (1994). *A fresh look at writing.* Portsmouth, NH: Heinemann.

Ord, J. (1998). *Kids from Kanata.* Retrieved from http://www.kidsfromkanata.org/~KFK

Sayers, D. (1991). Cross-cultural exchanges between students from the same culture: A portrait of an emerging relationship mediated by technology. *Canadian Modern Language Review, 47*(4), 678–696.

Smith, F. (1983, November). *The promise and threat of microcomputers for language learners.* Paper presented at the Annual Convention of Teachers of English to Speakers of Other Languages, Toronto, Ontario, Canada.

Sudol D., & Sudol, P. (1991). Another story: Putting Graves, Calkins, and Atwell into practice and perspective. *Language Arts, 68*(4), 292–300.

Westervelt, L. (1998). *Teaching writing using the process-oriented approach* (Report No. CS-216380). East Lansing, MI: National Center for Research on Teacher Learning. (ERIC Document Reproduction Service No. ED420864)

CHAPTER 9

Unraveling the Fear of Poetry/Reveling in the Pleasure of Poetry

CARL LEGGO

> A poet stands before reality that is every day new, miraculously complex, inexhaustible, and tries to enclose as much of it as possible in words. (Milosz, 1983, p. 56)
>
> I credit it [poetry] because credit is due to it, in our time and in all time, for its truth to life, in every sense of that phrase. (Heaney, 1995, p. 12)

I am a poet and a teacher. My poetry informs my teaching, and my teaching informs my poetry. I am an evangelical poet who preaches the good news that poetry is fundamental to our well-being. Yet, sadly, I also must claim to be a lonely poet because our contemporary world mostly ignores poets, and a lonely teacher of poetry because poetry writing is often neglected in classrooms. Teachers and students seem to be afraid of poetry. Often I hear comments such as "I never read poetry"; "I can't understand poetry"; "I can't imagine writing a poem."

Through facilitating school and community poetry workshops, pursuing research projects, and teaching undergraduate and graduate courses at the University of British Columbia, I work with a wide range of students from kindergartners to senior citizens. Like many students of all ages that I talk to, I never wrote poetry in school. I believed that poetry was written by men who once lived in faraway countries, and I believed that poetry was only about significant themes of war and love and nature. I also thought that poetry had to be obscure, convoluted, and ambiguous—a kind of puzzle for deciphering, a puzzle that I could never solve. I, like many students I talk to, was led to believe that poetry is only written by singularly gifted people with special talents for rhyme and rhythm, insight and wisdom, and I was convinced that I had no such gifts.

I came to poetry only in my late 20s. During a time of personal crisis, I began to write in a journal, and I began to hear a vibrant voice in my writing that I had never heard before. Then I started to write poetry, and I discovered that I had much I wanted—even needed—to say about my daily life and world. Above all, I discovered that I love to revel in the possibilities of language. Now, I seek to encourage my students to write poetry as a way to know their worlds and as a way to be and become in the world. In this chapter, I share my experiences and insights on how to untangle the knots of fear of writing poetry and lack of recognition of the poets inside all students and teachers. Of all the genre of texts that students are invited to write in classrooms, I think the most ignored, even feared, is poetry. As a poet and teacher, I want to unravel the fear of poetry in order to promote revelling in the pleasure of poetry.

What Is a Poem?

This knot of fear that requires untangling begins with addressing the question, What is a poem? One of my main goals in teaching the writing of poetry is to deconstruct the many misconceptions about poetry. A poem does not have to rhyme, and a poem does not have to be obscure and ambiguous, nor does it need to be about grand themes like love, war, and religion. I claim that a poem can be about anything and everything; I claim that the world is filled with poems. A poem is written out of engagement with the world and engagement with words. Therefore, I always begin with the question, What is a poem?

Too often, readers and writers, especially young readers and writers, are intimidated by the self-conscious fear that a poem is a text that only can be composed or deciphered by people with rare gifts of creativity and intellect. But, I stress that readers and writers are always performing poetic texts. There is no hidden meaning that must be revealed. The poetic text is a site where readers and writers engage in unique and creative performances from their imaginations and understandings, their experiences and emotions. The poetic text is not a puzzle to be laboriously pieced together but a stage on which to perform in a plurality of responses and approaches. There can be no univocal, authoritative reading or writing of a poem. To gain this understanding, students need exposure to a wide range of poetry, including found, sound, concrete, and prose poems. One of the main reasons I love poetry is that the genre is so inexhaustibly capacious. The question, What is a poem? cannot be answered definitively. Poets are always pushing the boundaries of poetry, establishing new edges and inviting new possibilities.

Of the many barriers that inhibit poetry writing in classrooms, none is more formidable than the set of expectations that students bring to the experience of reading and writing poetry. Strenski and Esposito (1980) explored the expectations of their students in an innovative research project with some startling conclusions. They asked their students to read two unsigned poems, one "generated at random by a computer, in turn based on a program of components blindly selected from anthologies" (p. 142) and one by poet Philip Levine. The students read and evaluated the poems. Strenski and Esposito were alarmed with the students' misconceptions about poetry. For example, the students expressed their convictions that "only some subjects are suitable for poetry" and that "a conversational or intimate tone is inappropriate" and that "poetry must be correctly punctuated" and "must have regular rhythm" (pp. 145–146). Even more disturbing for Strenski and Esposito was that "students...heard confusion in the computer poem, called it ambiguity, and met it with awe and respect. If they could not understand, the fault was theirs. Unintelligibility equalled profundity equalled better than they" (p. 149).

Much of the difficulty students have with reading and writing poetry is that they bring inappropriate and inadequate expectations and views to their understanding of poetry. Therefore, in order to expand and enlarge students' comprehension of the possibilities of poetry, their expectations and views must be enlarged and expanded. To help achieve that goal, students need exposure to a wide variety of poems, as well as frequent opportunities to write poetry.

Nurturing Writers and Writing

There are no formulaic approaches that guarantee success in writing, but there are many ways to nurture writing and writers. Since the early 1970s, writing instruction in schools has focused on the writing process model, which emphasizes an experience with writing that invites and encourages students to understand themselves as real writers writing about subjects that are personally relevant in order to communicate with real audiences. (See chapter 1 for a more detailed description of the writing process model.) Many of the ideas that support the writing process model have been adapted from the experiences and wisdom of professional writers (Atwell, 1998; Graves, 1989; Graves & Stuart, 1985; Murray, 1985, 1990).

However, there are serious concerns that the cultural context of the school classroom is not conducive to the contexts in which professional writers write. Parsons (1994) observes, "Schools, at best, offer a difficult, almost hostile, environment for writers. Restrictions, distractions, and a variety of contradictory pressures not only complicate but actually militate against the writing process" (p. 41). He adds, "Professional writers write in the real world. Students write (and teachers teach) in the tangled, frustrating, and sometimes baffling world of schools" (pp. 42–43). I take Parsons's concern seriously, but I do not agree with him. As a writing teacher in classrooms, I am always informed by my experiences as a writer. Therefore, I teach writing as a poet, and my delight in poetry inspires all my teaching. Moreover, I am sure that all teachers and students can know personally the delights of poetry. In classrooms, we need to read, write, hear, discuss, and publish poetry, and we need to recognize daily that all of us are poets with a keen sense of the creative dynamics of language. In classrooms, teachers and students can read a wide range of poems; compile portfolios of favorite poems; celebrate poetry with music, drama, and art; and invite other poets to visit. Every classroom can be a place where poetry is simply but consistently acknowledged as integral to living well in the world.

Recently, I read a wonderful book that represents the spirit of my approaches to reading and writing poetry. Creech's (2001) *Love That Dog* is a novel written as a sequence of poems in which the narrator, a young student named Jack, learns about poetry. He begins on September 13 with the following words:

September 13
I don't want to
because boys
don't write poetry.
Girls do. (p. 1)

Introduced by his teacher, Miss Stretchberry, to poems by William Carlos Williams, Robert Frost, William Blake, Valerie Worth, Arnold Adoff, S.C. Rigg, and Walter Dean Myers, Jack explores the images and sounds of poetry, the craft of writing poems, and the way that line breaks and shapes on the page evoke pictures in the imagination; above all, Jack learns how poems resonate with the memories, emotions, and experiences of his life. During the school year, Jack listens to, reads, and composes poems, all the time questioning the limits of poetry, discovering in the process that poetry constantly contravenes limits while always staying close and connected to the heart.

Similar to Jack in *Love That Dog* learning the lively pleasures of poetry, all students can be invited to attend to poetry as breathing, singing, and imagining everyday experiences and emotions in words that connect them to the world.

All Writing Creates/All Writing Is Created

Hanging over the desk in my office is a poster of the alphabet. I put the 26 letters of the alphabet there to remind me that as a writer and a language educator, I work (and play) daily with the alphabet. These are the raw materials of my craft and art. Sometimes, I forget to see the alphabet; sometimes, I take the alphabet for granted. As de Kerckhove (1995) notes, "The alphabet is like a computer program, but more powerful, more precise, more versatile and more comprehensive than any software yet written. A program designed to run the most powerful instrument in existence: the human being" (p. 28). Writers write their worlds in words. With the resources of the alphabet we explore and express who we are in the world. The alphabet provides the building blocks for constructing knowledge about our identity both as individuals and in relationship with others. And de Kerckhove adds, "Writing down one's own thoughts, whether they concern oneself directly or are musings about reality or social observations, has the immediate consequence of defining one's relationship to reality and of reinforcing one's point of view on that reality" (p. 196).

As an initial writing exercise in poetry workshops, I invite my students from elementary school children to senior citizens to write down the 26 letters of the alphabet. Then, I ask them to circle their five favorite letters. Some students look surprised. Some say, "I've never thought about letters that way." After they have circled their five favorite letters, I ask them to write quickly five words that begin with each of the five favorite letters. Some students mumble that they wish they had not picked X. Next, I invite them to look through their list of 25 words for poems. Many are delighted with the music of alliteration and the zaniness of connections that they discover among the seemingly disparate words. In this brief introductory writing exercise, the students begin to look at the alphabet with heightened consciousness, and they catch glimpses of a wild energy that pulses in the process and experience of word making.

I emphasize the performative activity of language. Too often, we use language to declare, assert, prove, argue, convince, and proclaim notions of "truth." But what happens if we emphasize the use of language to question, play with, savor, and ruminate on notions of "truth"? Language as performance invites interactive responses—intellectual, emotional, spiritual, and aesthetic. Language as performance invites students to enter into the labyrinth of human knowing and being in order to learn that the labyrinth, apparently chaotic and undecipherable, is in fact an experience rich with possibilities. Students need to celebrate the diversity that inevitably characterizes human be(com)ings constituted in the play of language. Therefore, teachers and students need to be committed to writing and rewriting their stories together, and they need to be committed to hearing one another's stories, too. In this creative interaction, teachers and students will learn together the dynamic possibilities of writing their lives in diverse and complex ways.

This understanding of how language is performative reminds me that the expression "creative writing" is redundant because all writing creates and all writing is created. Writing and creation are one. Much of my current thinking about writing has been inspired and informed by the words of Barthes (1989) who, in particular, discusses the ways that writing creates even as writing is created. Barthes reminds teachers that writers are both subject and object, active and passive, writing and written: I write, therefore, I am; I am written, therefore, I am. On the one hand, Barthes explains writing in terms of the active agency of writers:

> To write is today to make oneself the center of the action of speech, it is to effect writing by affecting oneself, to make action and affection coincide, to leave the *scriptor* inside the writing—not as a psychological subject..., but as agent of the action. (p. 18)

But at the same time, Barthes is quick to note how language actively creates the writer:

> Language cannot be considered as a simple instrument—utilitarian or decorative—of thought. Man does not exist prior to language, either as a species or as an individual. We never encounter a state where man is separated from language, which he then elaborates in order to "express" what is happening within him: it is language which teaches the definition of man, not the contrary. (pp. 12–13)

And so, Barthes encourages teachers to question the act and activity of writing, the intersections of writer and writing.

Elbow's (1981) suggestions about freewriting also are important to teachers who want students to break out of stereotypical ways of writing poetry. Elbow recommends that a writer begin with freewriting: "To do a freewriting exercise, simply force yourself to write without stopping for ten minutes" (p. 13). Elbow claims,

Freewriting makes writing easier by helping you with the root psychological or existential difficulty in writing: finding words in your head and putting them down on a blank piece of paper. So much writing time and energy is spent not writing: wondering, worrying, crossing out, having second, third, and fourth thoughts. (p. 14)

I suggest that teachers invite their students to begin their poetry writing with a remembered image, word, or thought that in turn generates a freewriting exercise. I find that it is helpful to get a block of words on the white page. Then I have something concrete to react to, to question, to listen to, to expand and compress, and to shape and sculpt. Freewriting is a way of thinking on paper, a way of letting words surprise the writer. What often happens in freewriting is that the conscious mind loses some of its control, and suddenly long-forgotten memories surface. Connections between events that have been little understood emerge, and emotions that are often suppressed laugh and cry out. Above all, freewriting is a way of tapping into the energy of words and word making.

Teachers can encourage students' divergent and creative and critical thinking in many other ways, too. Some writing strategies for getting started promote a haphazard approach, while other strategies promote a structured approach. I think that different writers need different strategies at different times, while engaging in different kinds of writing experiences. Student writers need to know that writing is an organic process that is integrally connected to their experiences, emotions, and observations. Above all, students need to know that writing can be fun and fulfilling. I offer the following suggestions for getting started and writing poetry in hopes that writers, beginning and experienced, will revel in the many possibilities for poem making.

Babble and Doodle:
Suggestions for Writing Poetry

In addition to freewriting, some other strategies for getting started are brainstorming, mapping, charting, drawing, doodling, dancing, outlining, questioning, talking, role-playing, making lists, taking notes, meditating, drawing analogies, writing in a journal, remembering, and conducting impromptu debates. The goal of these activities is to foster creative exploration. I like Lindemann's (1987) advice:

Students should view prewriting activities, not as isolated events, but as parts of a process that always looks ahead to drafting and revising. There are ways to let a piece of writing grow, ways to let us find a topic but also to let the topic find us. (p. 92)

I often begin a writing class with what I call the WWF (World Writing Federation) Competition. In order to focus students' attention, I write on the board or call out a sentence, such as, "I ran through the shopping mall in my pajamas." Then, with me using a stopwatch to time exactly three minutes, everybody writes. The goal is to write as many words as possible. I tell my students, "You do not need to be concerned about handwriting, punctuation, or even making sense. The only goal is to write as many words as you can in three minutes." The WWF Champion is the writer with the most words. In this playful way, we warm up for writing and invite the energy of words to fill our classroom.

I sometimes invite students to "Wander for Wonder," and we wander in a familiar place and record in a journal any observations or uses of language or images that catch our attention. I remind them that it is important to realize that there is wonder all around us. Also, I invite students to engage in scavenger hunts for interesting uses of language on billboards, bumper stickers, T-shirts, and refrigerator magnets, and to observe human behavior by sitting in a public place and recording in a notebook all the odd and eccentric things they see and hear. Sometimes they complete sentence stems, such as "I wonder...," "I remember...," "War is...," "I hope...," "Love is...." A further way I seek to stimulate imaginative and vibrant thinking and writing is to invite my students to seek connections among disparate items. For example, I ask, "How many uses can you dream up for a Coca-Cola bottle, a rubber band, a toilet plunger, and a cheese grater?"

One exercise that I have used with very young students in elementary classrooms and participants in senior citizens' writing groups is "Ping Pong." I invite small groups of four or five students to use just the two words *ping* and *pong* to write a poem. I direct them with just a few words of advice: You can change the order of the letters in the two words and you can repeat the letters and words without limit, but you cannot use any other letters. After composing your poem, use an overhead or poster paper to display the poem, or perform the group poem in an oral and dramatic presentation. I am always fascinated with the poems that are generated. I have seen young children compose poems that visually represent a ping pong table, ball, and paddles. I have heard others perform exquisite songs about pigs that bounce like kangaroos. The possibilities seem endless.

With this exercise, I introduce students to my conviction that a poem is basically babble and doodle (Leggo, 1997). Everything in a poem that appeals to the ears—the sense of hearing—is babble, including rhyme, rhythm, alliteration, consonance, onomatopoeia, and everything in a poem that appeals to the eyes—the sense of seeing—is doodle, including imagery, similes, metaphors, layout on the page, shape, and stanzaic structure. I invite students to compose concrete or visualist poems so the shape, design, or layout on the page illustrates the subject of the poem. A concrete or visualist poem emphasizes the doodle of poetry and often militates against an oral reading. I invite my students to write sound poems, too. For example, in small groups students compose poems that represent the sounds of a machine, the wind, the sea, a busy city street, or a snowstorm. Sound poems emphasize the babble of poetry and invite oral performances. In addition to concrete and sound poems, I introduce students to found poems and encourage them to look for poems everywhere. For example, I encourage them to find a portion of text (for example, washroom graffiti, memos from the principal's office, bumper stickers, newspaper headlines, milk cartons, rule-books for basketball), and shape the words into a poem. Some people ask, Is a found poem really a poem? I respond that there are millions of poems just waiting to be found.

Above all, I want students to have fun with poetry. So, I invite them to write doughnut poems by brainstorming all the names of doughnuts that they can think of, all the words that come to mind when they think about doughnuts, or by visiting a local doughnut shop and writing down all the names of doughnuts that they find. Then they use these words to write or draw doughnut poems. Perhaps the poem can be done in small groups on big sheets of art paper with colored markers and pastels. I invite them to make up their own names for doughnuts, even to draw and write the most appetizing and the most nauseating doughnuts they can. In related strategies, I invite students to compose color poems by listing all the memories and associations connected with a particular color—red or blue perhaps—followed by shaping the words into poems by selecting the memories and associations that are personally most significant. Or, I invite students to compose a flower poem by writing down all the names of flowers that they can recall or find through research and then shaping the names into a poem.

I encourage students to play with rhyme by listing all the words that rhyme with *pig*, *tree*, or *sky* and to write list poems by making lists of everything they like and dislike, or everything they remember and do not remember. I ask them to compile a poster poem by cutting headlines and bits of text and pictures from magazines and newspapers and composing them on Bristol board in order to present a theme such as ecology or violence. Always, I invite my students to understand that poetry is a flexible and wide-ranging genre and to experiment with the possibilities.

I also introduce my students to double-voiced poems, and they compose poems that combine two voices, such as the voice they use in public and the inner voice that speaks in their heads but is not often made public. A double-voiced poem weaves two texts that are related. The alternating lines can be written in boldface or italics or different colors of ink to suggest the two voices. My students also investigate the poetry of popular song lyrics, advertising jingles, and greeting cards, and they write their own lyrics, jingles, and cards. Also, while I encourage my students to explore traditional poetic forms, such as the sonnet, cinquain, haiku, villanelle, ghazal, tanka, ode, elegy, and limerick, I remind them frequently that poetry is so flexible that there is always room for inventing new forms.

Conclusion

Writing poetry cannot be taught like a paint-by-numbers kit. There are no easy formulas for learning to write poetry. Writers are individuals and, therefore, must be given opportunities to grow as writers in their own ways. Different writers will need different approaches to writing. The basic question that needs to be asked over and over about a writing approach is, Does it accomplish the goal of nurturing writers and their writing?

I am committed to nurturing writers filled with desire, writers who take risks in their meaning-making, revel in the wonder of words, and know that they weave their worlds as they weave their words and as words weave them in worlds spilling and spelling without end.

SPELL POETRY
a long time ago
I saw a birch tree
hold the late winter
light of afternoon
after rain left
even the ducks
in the slough
sopping mad

like once
or maybe twice
I have seen
lovers hold
the love
of the other
in their eyes
and now
in this poem
I walk the dike
again, see again
the birch tree
holds still
the late winter
light of afternoon:

I spell my words
on the page;
I am caught
in the spell.

If I learn
to spell poetry,
will I know
the spell of poetry?

REFERENCES

Atwell, N. (1998). *In the middle: New understandings about writing, reading and learning.* Portsmouth, NH: Heinemann.

Barthes, R. (1989). *The rustle of language* (R. Howard, Trans.). Berkeley, CA: University of California Press.

de Kerckhove, D. (1995). *The skin of culture: Investigating the new electronic reality.* Toronto: Somerville House.

Elbow, P. (1981). *Writing with power: Techniques for mastering the writing process.* New York: Oxford University Press.

Graves, D.H. (1989). *Experiment with fiction.* Portsmouth, NH: Heinemann.

Graves, D.H., & Stuart, V. (1985). *Write from the start: Tapping your child's natural writing ability.* New York: New American Library.

Heaney, S. (1995). *Crediting poetry: The Nobel lecture.* Loughcrew, Ireland: Gallery Press.

Leggo, C. (1997). *Teaching to wonder: Responding to poetry in the secondary classroom.* Vancouver, BC: Pacific Educational Press.

Lindemann, E. (1987). *A rhetoric for writing teachers* (2nd ed.). New York: Oxford University Press.

Milosz, C. (1983). *The witness of poetry.* Cambridge, MA: Harvard University Press.

Murray, D.M. (1985). *A writer teaches writing* (2nd ed.). Boston: Houghton, Mifflin.

Murray, D.M. (1990). *Shoptalk: Learning to write with writers.* Portsmouth, NH: Boynton/Cook.

Parsons, L. (1994). *Expanding response journals in all subject areas.* Markham, ON: Pembroke.

Strenski, E., & Esposito, N.G. (1980). The poet, the computer, and the classroom. *College English, 42,* 142–150.

LITERATURE CITED

Creech, S. (2001). *Love that dog.* New York: HarperCollins.

CHAPTER 10

The Tangle of Context: Making Meaning by Writing in Role

DAVID BOOTH

> Dear King,
>
> My people in the village below you hear you are making a fountain in front of your castle, and we also hear it will take up all the water for our pets, our produce and us. Your town, which soon faces destruction, is asking you if you would stop the building of the fountain. If you refuse, we have some reasons why you should reconsider. Most of the people are too old to walk twenty miles to get the water that their families need. The students don't know the way to the east and the wild animals might get them. The merchants want more money for getting the water and they want the poor to pay for it. Please don't build the fountain. You won't regret it.
>
> Jeremy (9 years old)

This powerful and carefully constructed letter was written by a fourth-grade student working in role with his class during a drama unit based on the themes in Alexander's (1989) picture book *The King's Fountain*. After sharing the story, the teacher organized a role-playing situation in which five students working as the king's emissaries brought the news to the remaining students, in roles of the villagers, that the king was going to build a fountain for the glory of his kingdom and that it would require all the water from the village. The ensuing discussion grew very emotional, and the teacher asked the villagers to work in groups and write down their thoughts and feelings in letters to the king. The king's emissaries acted as scribes, and the documents were then revised to the standards demanded by a king and copied onto beautiful parchment paper with calligraphy pens. The resulting letters were works of art, but for me, their greatest significance lay in the words and sentence structures the "villagers" had chosen in order to effect a change in the king's thinking. Something had altered the everyday writing of these children.

One of the knotty issues in the teaching of writing is finding classroom contexts that support meaningful and authentic writing experiences.

Some classroom writing events do not help students deal with inner compulsion or a strongly felt need to express themselves, but often focus on the completion of assignments. However, when writing is embedded in a context that has personal significance for the writer (Graves, 1994; Wells, 2001), writing potential can be increased. The writer can explore meaning making through both content and form. If students are engaged in the expressive and reflective aspects of drama and live through "here and now" experiences that draw from their own life meanings, the writing that grows from the drama may possess the same characteristics and qualities.

Research on Drama and Writing

The connections between drama and writing are in the literature on the teaching of drama (Ackroyed, 2000; Gallagher, 2000; Wagner, 1998). My own work in drama-influenced writing has been strengthened by a yearlong research project codirected by British drama educator Jonothan Neelands and funded by the Toronto District School Board (Booth & Neelands, 1998). The teachers and schools involved in the project volunteered to monitor and record the writing activity done by their classes in response to drama. The explicit goal of the project was to "explore the effect of drama on the writing development of young adolescents in inner city settings over a six month period" (Booth & Neelands, 1998, p. iii). All the teachers involved had prior experience as teachers of drama and regularly looked for opportunities for introducing writing assignments as part of the drama curriculum. The student cohort represented a wide range of abilities and included a significant number of ESL students. (For further reading on supporting ESL and L2 students' writing, see chapters 5 and 6.) The teachers were supported by external researchers who observed the teaching, took part in the teaching themselves, and conducted in-depth ethnographic interviews with groups of students involved in the project. The research reinforced the contributions that drama can offer students planned opportunities to engage with a broad range of writing genres in their classroom work.

The students from grades 7, 8, and 9 who were involved in the project offered their reactions in a variety of modes, from journals to interviews:

> In English you're so worried about all these things; you want content, but you need grammar. In drama, first it's the content, second you can go back and correct your spelling. The difference between doing writing in drama and doing writing in English is that in English they mostly give us topics, but when we're in drama we usually get to pick what we want to do. We just write

what we feel like writing and just keep on writing. We tend to write more than in other classes.

In my English class we have this assignment where we have to write a letter, as if we were someone who was in a short story. Doing the same sort of thing in drama I thought that there was much more feeling in it, since I had acted it out. And I'm sure if I thought back to English, if I thought that, "Okay, you think I'm this person and I'm writing so this would be different." It was the same assignment but two different approaches.

When we're writing we listen to things other people have said and borrow them, and everybody uses something different. It's partly to do with being able to take everybody else's ideas and put them together with our own. It's kind of like brainstorming. It makes the story a lot better.

The drama helps us with our writing. We get to find out how the character feels, things that we haven't thought of before. You get more in the drama to write about.

The Centre for Language in Primary Education, located in London, England, completed a two-year research project to examine the changes that take place in students' writing when they study challenging literature, and to note which classroom practices support students in learning about writing from literary texts. The results (Barrs & Cork, 2001) reveal the power of drama in opening up topics for writing and for extending and deepening the contexts for writing in different genres.

Where students are writing in role, out of a fictional situation in which they have been able to explore and discuss thoroughly, they are able to access areas of language and feeling that they might not normally be thought to be aware of. Writing in role seemed to be a way of developing and building on students' insights into the human experiences that fictions are based on. Often in this kind of writing students seemed to be "trying on" mature experience, thinking their way into the responsibilities, cares, joys, and griefs of adulthood. The writing in role offered them the opportunity of becoming, in the words of Vygotsky's description of dramatic play, "a head taller."

Students seemed to have been helped to enter the world of the story by the role-play within the drama. This piece of writing sometimes led to a shift in the case study students' writing; for instance students filled in more imagined detail around the narrative, in a way that had obviously been encouraged by the drama. Writing in role seemed to be, as already reported, a real aid to students' progress as writers.

In most classrooms it led to writing which was thoroughly imagined and qualitatively different from what had gone before. This finding has implications for the place of drama in the language arts curriculum, and points to the value of enabling students to "live through" fictions by involving them in different forms enactment. (p. 213)

Connecting Writing and Drama

The experience of deeply felt drama can affect writing in so many ways. When students work in role inside invented worlds and unfamiliar contexts, their perspectives may change. Because drama is an art form that progresses in the classroom just as a story does on paper, the process of drama is similar to that of writing. When students move from drama to writing and base their ideas on these firsthand, lived-through role playing experiences, they can bring new insight and involvement to their interactions with language. Writing in role, or as a result of role-playing, lets students of all ages adopt a new set of attitudes and feelings generated by the role, and at the same time, lets them keep their own in mind. Through the process of writing, participants can give form to their feelings and ideas and learn not only to express their views but also to reexamine and reassess themselves in light of the intended audience (readers or listeners) and their needs. They begin to think of themselves as writers who control the medium in order to say what they want. Writing generated in response to the concrete particulars of a drama context can be connected to real human situations and not only considered as classroom practice. In role playing situations, the relationship of talk and writing can be emphasized, with language, thought, and feeling experienced as a whole. We write to see what we might say, to see what others will think about our thoughts, or to examine what we think we have said.

Educating the imagination can be a slow process when students work in the written mode. However, drama is a catalyst that the teacher can use to help students tap resources that they may not have known were there. As students enter into problems and conflicts in role, constructed through the drama exploration, they imagine themselves as other people, thinking their thoughts and feeling their responses. They begin to view situations from outside themselves and see the consequences of their actions from a new perspective. Once the setting is in their mind's eye and reflected in the lives of the characters they have created, they often can transfer these processes to their writing. Imaginative involvement in drama can be a powerful stimulus for writing, and that writing in turn can serve several different purposes in the drama work. The best drama, and the most effective opportunities for linking writing with it, emerge over extended periods during which students have time and the incentive to work their way into an intensive and extensive unit of work, to refocus and change direction, and to edit and present their creations to trusted and understanding others.

In their role-generated writing, students can use their imaginations to travel further into the dramatic situation and let meanings that have accrued in the shadows of the drama reveal themselves. As they try for a more elaborate, imaginative understanding of the events of the drama, their writing and their language use become more complex.

Writing Within the Drama Context

Drama can act as a strong prewriting activity, from creating journals and letters to drawing diagrams and brainstorming lists that can then set the scene for the drama work. In addition, the written texts can act as significant artifacts within the situation to be explored in role. The drama lesson itself can involve written language in a variety of forms: writing letters in role; creating announcements, proclamations, and petitions; reporting about events within the drama and in reflective journals; designing advertisements and brochures; inventing questionnaires and important documents; and writing narrative stories that are part of or conjured up by the drama. In addition, there are many opportunities for collective writing, in which groups collaborate on a mutual enterprise. For example, students can cooperate as scientists in collecting data, as aliens organizing information, or as villagers writing to the king. Students are then revising and editing in role—inside the drama context.

As teachers work in role within the drama activity, perhaps as a member of the fictional community such as a reporter or a villager, they also can participate in the variety of writing events that are integral to the drama. For example, in one lesson I observed, the teacher's sensitive contribution in role, concerning the letter a group was writing to the village council, deepened and strengthened the impact of the subsequent drama events, as the powerful letter, read aloud, intensified the mood of the participants. The teacher's careful intervention, while working in role, supported and focused the students' writing.

Writing Drawn From the Drama Experience

Writing after the drama experience provides opportunities for students to revisit and rethink the issues and concerns raised in the drama. They can begin to analyze the motives and behaviors that emerged during the drama and seek reasons and implications for assumptions and decisions they made while in role. The thought, the discussion, and the writing that occur after the drama may be as important to students' learning as what happened during the action. As the students look back on what they have done, we often can find ways to make the learning that has occurred explicit by questioning and deepening their reflections on the implications and consequences of their actions in role. Students can use the reflective composing time in unique ways as they attempt to tell what had happened, investigate motivation for the actions of the characters, or ponder the reasons for the results of the whole interactive process. The drama provides contexts for the writing, and the writing illuminates the drama work. The impact of the drama made visible by the process of writing can lead to the students' more universal understanding of their world.

Prompted by the drama experience, the students can reflect in their writing by clarifying and interpreting their thoughts and feelings as they replay and rework the events and the possibilities that have been opened up through the dramatic exploration. One teacher noted the student ownership that can result from writing generated by the action and involvement of drama work: "It takes significant experience to create good writing, and this was their story they created in drama, rather than my story and my expectations. I think that really made the difference."

When I work in role alongside the students, I find that my students and I can verbalize and mediate our feelings in our writing. As students write their own versions of what happened, they can redefine their experiences through discussion and comparison in groups with others, becoming active "storyers" who begin to understand themselves as both writers and role-players. I need to read what they write, after they are freed from the imperatives of my lessons and are back in their owned space. They attempt to talk to me through their writing but often resort to talking to themselves through the medium of the poem or the letter, thinking with a pen or a mouse, while at the same time altering forever my personal meaning making from our time together. I see the drama through different lenses because I have read what they have written; they have reconsidered their own experiences through reflective distancing and "remembered role" (Booth, 1994, p. 7). My drama work alters as their writing informs me about their perceptions of what has occurred. These students in the middle years, ages 12 to 14, seem to grasp the effect of drama on their composing:

> Instead of just doing research and then trying to imagine a story based on that, doing drama using your research first makes story writing more real.

You can base it on the things that happened to you in drama, which are like the things that happen to you in life, and you're learning at the same time.

Doing the drama first helps writing because in drama. You get to use a lot of your imagination, and so you're thinking for yourself, and then when you go back into English class you can use what you've done in drama to help.

In English, normally the teacher will just say, "Okay, write about this." And if you want to put something else into the story, you can't. But with drama, you can use your whole imagination, you can put whatever you want into the story and it's yours. It's not the teacher's.

You get this feeling of writing; you want to express yourself, and you really want to get into this character, and you're going really deep into this character. And it's good. You don't get the same "wanting to write" in English.

As a result of working with drama, my understanding of how a story is written, or how a story is made, or how a piece of writing works—just the way that writing is put together has changed. I tend to pay more attention to the human side now. Before I didn't put a lot of dialogue in my writing, and now I'm starting to include more, because I feel it's more important to get the reactions of the people as they respond to each other.

As I review and reflect on my own work in drama and writing inside classrooms, the "remembered role" recurs as the strategy most frequently chosen by the students themselves as they revisit their experiences with the shared story and the playmaking activities. They attempt to make sense of what has happened, still inside the memory of their roles, drawing from the spectator/participant relationship of those who were involved in real pretending, which is, of course, the heart of childhood play. The writing that grows from "remembered role" may reveal much more about the students and their experiences than traditional reflective discussions built around the questions of what did they like or what did they not like. Supporting the development of emotional intelligence includes creating and sustaining opportunities for reflective consideration as the students move on with their lives. Reflection offers a chance to be heard, an opportunity to express ideas and feelings, and an occasion for language.

Partly as the result of deliberate interventions by skilled drama teachers, partly as a response to what the students in the study were trying to do in their meaning making, features of dramatic role play appeared in their writing, especially when the writer adopted a different role as the narrator. It is important to note that this is not the same activity as writing in the first person. Most apprentice writers can be encouraged to become authors by generating a text about themselves. To write as someone else is to accomplish a kind of reflexivity, me, yet not me, peculiar to authors. (Barrs & Cork, 2001, p. 12)

The drama that the students have experienced gives them ideas for writing, and that writing in turn can be used for sharing their insights about what they have experienced. Revealing our understanding of drama through writing lets us then link two vital processes together. The drama work also generates metaphoric and analogous writing that may be deeply influenced by the role-playing and by the communicative experiences embedded in the work. While drama is an active, "doing" medium, the reflective mode "allows students to make meaning by examining and understanding their thoughts and reflection" as Bolton (1984, p. 23) says. This meaning making transpires when students relate the information and feelings gleaned from a drama experience to another situation. This generalization may occur much later or be revealed informally in a seemingly unrelated context. As one teacher commented,

> What I found with particular students was that the drama really seemed to kick-start their writing in other areas as well. It seemed to give them the confidence and the liberation so that they would even choose to write when it wasn't mandatory or time to write. They would just sit and write. One boy in particular wrote as a response to a film in a way that I'd never seen him write before. And I think that the drama really helped him.

Conclusion

Neelands and I drew the following conclusions from our study of writing in role (Booth & Neelands, 1998), and our findings are similar to Barrs and Cork's (2001) summaries from the British project, and are supported by Wagner's (1998) research in the United States:

- It is significant that student comments about the worthiness of a piece of writing generally relate to argumentative, opinion-giving letters, articles, or statements. Not to be overlooked are the psychosocial effects and impact of this type of drama work. Stepping into someone else's shoes, sharing new and different perspectives from the ones usually assumed is also a self-reflective activity and may generate strong reactions from students as they come up against their own false assumptions and prejudices, often for the first time. Writing is a transformative activity.
- Writing in role affords the opportunity for the students to put their responses into the character and then step back and examine that response without excessive risk-taking and the need for heavy

defenses to be raised. In this manner, drama-related writing provides opportunities for psychosocial growth that is not available in more traditional structured writing activities. Socialization is central to the purpose of schooling, a responsibility of school boards and educators and another component of the moral purpose of writing in drama.

- Characterization work in drama enhances the students' sense of character and voice in their writing. When interviewed, students in all classes commented on the depth of character they could produce in their writing if the characters had been fleshed out for them through improvisation. Within these improvisations, students had to imaginatively explore and use the gestures and language that they felt were appropriate to their characters.

- The experience of taking on a character in drama also provided many students with enhanced empathy and understanding for a broad range of people. In turn, this allowed them to write sensitively and genuinely from a variety of different viewpoints. In many of the drama themes in their classes, students were invited to take on several roles that often had conflicting values or positions on an issue. Following the drama, students had writing assignments that encouraged them to use an unfamiliar voice to present different sides of an argument. They found this aspect of drama useful to the development of their writing and also commented on drama's usefulness in challenging stereotyping and prejudice, because students work in a variety of roles, each role requiring different perspectives.

- The findings concerning the effect of the drama and writing on the students' appreciation of their perspectives suggest strongly the relationship of drama to other areas of the curriculum (social studies, family studies, problem solving, etc.).

The teaching of writing will always be a complex, multifaceted process full of worrisome knots. How we go about helping young writers first to select those issues that matter to them and that offer possibilities for thoughtful, written development, and then to assist and guide them as they work out and through their jumble of ideas—these are the tangles. Drama-inspired writing offers strong opportunities for writing events that are driven by the needs of the students to construct their thoughts and feelings into print texts. For me, the following two student reflections sum up the possibilities inherent in teaching experiences that have incorporated role-generated writing in the learning:

> A broader understanding gets built by being in the shoes of other people, and having to think like other people. By learning things in situations that are happening, most people don't listen when people tell them things. And usually you always learn things the hard way. In a drama, even though you're not learning the hard lesson yourself you're putting yourself in the shoes of someone who's learning the hard lesson. And that makes you think and write better.

> It's like we're traveling through different places. We get different experiences we wouldn't otherwise have. In this class, we get the chance to feel how other people feel. Out of the kinds of experiences and feelings we had in drama, we wondered, "How do we change the way things are?" We've started to change things in our school, to be more aware of other people. It's also another way you can build respect, learning what these people have gone through. That's why we want to talk and to write to each other.

REFERENCES

Ackroyd, J. (2000). *Literacy alive: Drama projects for literacy learning.* London: Hodder & Stoughton.

Barrs, M., & Cork, V. (2001). *The reader in the writer.* London: Centre for Language in Primary Education.

Bolton, G.M. (1984). *Drama as education: An argument for placing drama at the center of the curriculum.* New York: Longman.

Booth, D. (1994). *Story drama: Reading, writing and role playing across the curriculum.* Markham, ON: Pembroke.

Booth, D., & Neelands, J. (1998). (Eds.). *Writing in role: Classroom projects connecting writing and drama.* Hamilton, ON: Caliburn.

Gallagher, K. (2000). *Drama education in the lives of girls: Imagining possibilities.* Toronto, ON: University of Toronto Press.

Graves, D.H. (1994). *A fresh look at writing.* Portsmouth, NH: Heinemann.

Wagner, B. (1998). *Educational drama and language arts: What research shows.* Portsmouth, NH: Heinemann.

Wells, G. (2001). *Dialogic inquiry: Towards a sociocultural practice and theory of education.* Cambridge, UK: Cambridge University Press.

LITERATURE CITED

Alexander, L. (1989). *The king's fountain.* New York: Dutton.

CHAPTER 11

Engaging Reluctant Adolescent Writers With Contemporary Literacy: Untangling Two Knots

JILL KEDERSHA MCCLAY

A idan (all students' names are pseudonyms) comments on his grade 8 *Hyperstudio* (Wagner, 1996) project, a teacher-assigned visual and text presentation on what he has learned as he has grown up. He compares this digital presentation to a more conventional essay:

> This way I had a lot of fun, and it was sort of complicated, but yet it was enjoyable. See, if I were to write an essay, I don't like writing essays because they're long and sometimes most of them are hard. And I find it very boring. So I wouldn't work on it as much.

Aidan helps me unravel two common knots in teaching writing: the knot of the reluctant, resistant, or even intractable young writer, and the knot of focusing sensibly on contemporary literacy in our teaching. I propose, paradoxically, that one knot can untie another—that working with new technologies and forms for writing can encourage reluctant adolescents to engage with writing. Singly, each of these knots represents a true difficulty in our teaching, but "intertwined," these two knots can be untangled. In this chapter, I suggest that teachers can engage reluctant adolescent writers by providing opportunities for them to work in contemporary literacy environments with newer multimedia technologies, to push boundaries in content and form, and to reconsider genuine writing processes.

We have been schooled to rely on a process approach to teaching writing (Atwell, 1998; Graves, 1994), with space for students to develop their own writing topics and through these topics, their individual voices. With reluctant young adolescent writers, however, the invitation to develop self-selected topics may be met with indifference or suspicion. Teachers, knowing the need to teach writing skills within the context of students' own writing, are understandably frustrated when they encounter young adolescents who resist writing. Writers must produce sustained text to make progress, and for reluctant writers a sentence or paragraph may test the limits of both students and teachers.

Although Aidan is not a reluctant writer, he often fails to complete language arts assignments. His comment raises points that are relevant for teachers who struggle to entice young adolescents to put fingers to the keyboard or pen to paper. Aidan indicates that he will invest effort in an assignment if it is "fun and complicated," as in the multimedia project. Work that is complicated is not a deterrent for Aidan if there is a suitable payoff. In further discussion, he makes it clear that there is "good complicated" and bad. "Good complicated" involves the challenge of working with a relatively unfamiliar (for him) multimedia program to present ideas visually and textually. A writer working with this program must decide how the interplay of visual and textual elements might work best—what should be said in text and what should be shown visually, how best to word the textual parts and how best to communicate other ideas visually and with some animation. If teachers want to help young adolescents become motivated writers, they need to structure writing opportunities that offer both fun and challenge.

Our contemporary literacy environment shows signs of what Dresang (1999) terms "radical change." Other researchers and teachers use terms such as "multiliteracies" (New London Group, 1996) or "new literacy" (Eisner, 1997) to call attention to the fact that what it means to be literate now involves a wider array of skills and behaviors than traditional print media alone require. Although we may argue in theory about how radical this shift truly is, classroom teachers cope with aspects of it on a daily basis when they face provincial or state mandates to integrate technology in their teaching and when they face adolescents whose literacy behaviors are not always recognized or valued in classrooms (Smith & Wilhelm, 2002).

The mandate for technology integration in curriculum bedevils teachers at all levels of schooling. Teachers struggle with the double task of learning to use the technology for themselves and of working out ways to use it in their teaching. Young adolescents seem "programmed" to understand much of this technology intuitively while adults fumble with it and crash hard drives. On the information superhighway, young adolescents are often the competent drivers, while adults may feel like the "crash-test dummies." To achieve the goal of sensible technology integration is not a simple exercise, however. We know that technology in and of itself does not entice young adolescents to compose because they are normally far less easy to impress and far quicker to see unadvertised possibilities in technology than are adults (Lewis, 2001). (For further information about the limitations and possibilities of using technology to write in classrooms, see chapter 8.)

Writing for the "Here and Now"—2003 Version

Ferreiro (2000), addressing the problem of functional illiteracy—of literate people who choose not to engage in literacy—stresses the importance of matching literacy demands in schools with the literacy demands that students meet in the world outside school. Her admonition suggests useful avenues for teachers to encourage reluctant writers. In the world outside school, the obvious literacy demands confronting adolescents and adults involve extensive use of multimedia and newer forms of writing. Teachers can use these newer media and forms to foster engagement with writing, but I want to caution again that technology is not in and of itself the answer to promote interest in writing. If the technology is not integral to the writing, students either will focus on the technology alone or quickly dismiss the technology. But, the intriguing aspect of many of the newer technologies and environments for writing is the question of how writers use them to create various literary and visual effects. Tchudi and Mitchell (1999) urge teachers to let students "write for the here and now." The "here and now" of literacy today abounds with multimedia.

When teachers align the literacy demands placed on adolescents in schools with the literacy demands that they meet in the world outside school, teachers look quickly to the Internet. Webpage design involves visual, auditory, and textual elements, often with text serving as the poor relation to the more immediate and attractive graphics and sound. By teaching students to work in multimedia forms, teachers can help them develop sensibilities for multimedia by working also with older, more traditional forms such as photography, picture books, and popular song. These traditional media provide more stable formats for examining some of the relationships between image and word or melody and word. With reluctant writers, the way into the text may well be through the visual or the auditory.

If teachers allow students to begin with the visual or auditory and move into text, they will help students work well with all elements. Students can begin by taking photographs. For example, they may experiment with black-and-white film to add a less familiar aspect to their work. The writing can proceed from the photo—about the photo, about what is just outside the lens, about the relative effects of black-and-white or color variation, or about the process of framing or developing the photo. Composing song lyrics, whether parodies or original creations, can foster understanding of rhythm and scansion in verbal phrasing because the repetition and beats in a melody help writers to focus on the oral qualities of their writing. As adolescents work in multimedia forms, they engage in asking real questions about which elements best contribute various effects. Written text must necessarily be concise and carefully presented, making revision more relevant and palatable.

While Ferreiro (2000), Dresang (1999), and others write of the literacy demands that students meet in the world around them, teachers of reluctant adolescent writers also do well to focus on literacy opportunities that are available. If teachers consider the popular culture world that their students inhabit, they can appreciate the literacy opportunities that many adolescents seek out so enthusiastically and that can help to unravel the knot of engaging reluctant writers. There is certainly no need, for example, for an adolescent to chat online with a friend who lives close by when a telephone call is so simple; nor is there any imperative for adolescents to post written comments to fan websites after the airing of their favorite television program. Yet, the attraction of AOL Instant Messenger and chat boards for any and all television shows is seemingly irresistible for many adolescents. Such written commentary has the advantages of audience and response—key elements for developing writing abilities. In addition, teachers who choose to open discussions about the situational appropriateness of language use in relation to such popular forums will perhaps do both teachers and students a great service.

Adolescent Boundary Pushing

In allowing students to develop topics of their own, teachers of adolescents may find themselves reading a few too many narratives or opinion pieces seemingly designed only to shock adult sensibilities. Such topics on the edges of classroom acceptability, whether intended to be frivolous or serious, can engage young writers. Adolescence is a time to push boundaries and to be subversive from a safe perch. Adolescent writers want to explore ideas that make adults uncomfortable. I do not advocate a boundary-free zone in school, but I feel that some leeway and examination of the social mores and tolerances of individuals and social groups will help students learn about the power of written language and how to define limits of acceptable language in diverse situations.

Smith, commenting on the lack of appeal of Canadian literature to young people, asserts, "What turns off young readers? A moral approach to literature. A lack of clever wickedness..." (as cited in Wright, 2001, p. 156). Much the same may be said for young writers when their writing is constrained by teachers who assign and accept only safe, inoffensive topics. Because adolescents need to push boundaries and find their voices, they learn by experience that words can be offensive and powerful. They need to give voice to their own "clever wickedness" and to resist their teachers' often "moral approach" to classroom writing. However, adolescents' desire to push boundaries, although motivating, does not need to rule out all other considerations in a classroom. One of the essential lessons of adolescence is the development of a sense of "other" both personally and in writing. As teachers encourage young people to write for varied audiences, they help their students develop an outward look, an ability to anticipate other people's perspectives and varied audiences' responses to writings. (I usually employ the "best friend" and "grandma" tests when discussing the appropriateness of diction with adolescents: Would you say it this way to your best friend? to your grandma? Which type of audience are you aiming at?) Young writers need to develop a sense of situational appropriateness to anticipate when and why some boundaries—of diction, of content, or of style—are transgressable, while others are not.

Teachers can provide some safe places for adolescents to explore and push boundaries. The teacher who provides clear guidance about what topics or treatments of topics are acceptable in his or her classroom—but is also willing to discuss and negotiate some of the minor boundary infringements—helps students learn to do the same. Young people gain in literacy and in knowledge of the world when teachers can position themselves more as guides and less as gatekeepers, as the following two examples from younger children and adolescents illustrate.

Example 1: The Adventures of Captain Underpants

In recent years, I have watched both with amusement and occasional frustration as *The Adventures of Captain Underpants* (Pilkey, 1997) phenomenon has played out in elementary schools. Pilkey's series unfolds in comic-book-within-a-story form as told by the mischievous characters George and Harold. In comic book form, the boys recount the adventures of superhero Captain Underpants (a.k.a., the school principal), who gives villains wedgies. Complete with bathroom humor, more fart jokes than most teachers really want to read, a gloriously irreverent attitude, and jokes that rely on the relationship of the visual to the verbal text, this series is a hit with both boys and girls. It has, to my knowledge, engaged at least a few previously reluctant readers, and it seems to inspire writing efforts that delight students and their classmates.

Sadly, Captain Underpants is also a series that some elementary teachers have banished from their classrooms. This is a lost opportunity, indeed. Young writers creating the "further adventures of..." can learn a great deal about textual and visual relationships because the comic book illustrations often subvert the seemingly innocent text. A reader who only reads the words misses the jokes. Young people can learn about the limits of bathroom humor and fart jokes (but their teachers also can learn something about the appeal of such) and about the concept of appropriateness in the context of a story. For example, one young writer who created his own Captain Underpants adventure engaged in a useful discussion with his teacher about the appropriateness (or lack thereof) of machine-gun fire in his story. Ultimately, he agreed with his teacher that such a level of violence was simply out of character in these stories, and he created instead a gun that shot bubble gum—more creative in its own right and more in keeping with the spirit of Pilkey's books. In this situation, the teacher did not impose an arbitrary "no violence" rule but worked within the context of a text that the student loved. In the process, the young writer displayed a "clever wickedness" that surpassed his initial desire merely to include violence in the story. Pilkey's own "clever wickedness" is also available on his website, http://www.pilkey.com, which offers helpful sections of "boring stuff for teachers" as well as "stuff for boring teachers."

Example 2: Making Up Megaboy

While many young children delight in the transgressions of bathroom humor in the Captain Underpants series, many adolescents enjoy stories that transgress the traditional boundaries of "safe" content for children. In adolescence, they are entering the world more knowingly, trying to make sense of an adult world to which they have substantial access in the media. They appreciate novels that speak directly to this exploration. *Making Up Megaboy* (Walter, 1998) challenges readers to make sense of a seemingly senseless act of violence: 13-year-old Robbie kills a Korean shopkeeper. Robbie has never been in trouble and has no apparent motive for his crime. The novel is told in multiple perspectives on double-page spreads, as each narrator (classmates, principal, parents, lawyer, social worker, etc.) relates his or her perspective on Robbie and on the crime, but Robbie never tells his own story. Readers must construct their own sense of what drove Robbie to this appalling act and what motivates each of the narrators.

The novel is a commentary on the treatment of violent episodes in contemporary mass media: Despite extensive, even excessive media attention, sensational events are not explained or illuminated clearly. Human motivation remains elusive. Readers are left to ponder whether the "whole truth" can possibly be revealed in mass media. The novel does not offer pat solutions or interpretations, a fact that unsettles some adult readers who want to take a more "moral approach" to literature for youth. Adolescents, however, are often quite eager to explore the implications of such commentary, as they see sensationalized news stories on a daily basis. Dresang (1999) quotes a sixth-grade reader of *Making Up Megaboy*: "The whole story is to make kids think. Adults think that kids just want everything to be straightforward, but kids like to think" (p. 244). Teachers who bring such engaging and challenging literature into classrooms have the ability to help young people think in depth about difficult issues, and such discussions will bridge naturally to their own writing.

Debates about the boundaries of taste and appropriateness lead easily and necessarily to a broader examination of some contentious social issues concerning language and literacy. Because it is easier to participate in the wider world now, by publishing or entering a conversation on the Internet, young people learn (sometimes the hard way) society's limits to free speech. Young people in online forums participate in boundary pushing, whether deliberately or accidentally. In recent years, teens have been held accountable for threats of violence and libelous statements on their personal websites and in classroom writing. At a less contentious level, they have been suppressed by media giant Time Warner, for example, who threatened legal action against adolescents' Harry Potter fan sites. Teachers must help students understand these issues because students do participate in the real, adult world of literacy, and such issues are far from being resolved.

Even if we only look to print media to encourage young writers, there are challenging contemporary works in traditional forms such as comic books and picture books. These forms, which adults often do not value highly for adolescents, are worth careful consideration. Picture books—

such as those created by Macaulay (1990, 1995) or Wiesner (2001)—comics, and graphic novels often involve intricate and sophisticated literacy demands in their interplay of graphic and textual elements and establishment of mood and tone (McCloud, 2000). Novels such as *Monster* (Myers, 1999) and *Making Up Megaboy* (Walter, 1998) mix genres and integrate graphic elements in intriguing ways. Introducing adolescents to these hybrid forms shows them possibilities for writing and illustrating and opens many productive avenues of exploration of text and image relationships. (See McClay, 2002, for a discussion of one adolescent's writing in hybrid forms.) They can serve as a link between traditional and electronic literacy (Lewis, 2001; Mackey & McClay, 2000), inviting young writers to consider text and images together. Picture books are highly accessible examples of polysemic codes, in which two or more symbol systems are at work simultaneously. From contemporary and challenging picture books, young writers can learn how authors push boundaries on the page. Such works often raise societal issues of concern to adolescents and can inspire mature consideration of challenging issues.

Engagement With Genuine Writing Processes and Evaluation

Teachers sometimes enshrine a sequence of writing process that does not relate to writers' actual work. Often, in my research with adolescent writers, the mismatch between the expected and the actual writing process shows most clearly in the realm of planning. Young people explain how they satisfy teachers' ideas about writing processes. Most commonly, they write a full draft first and then fake a planning sheet or concept map. Sarah is a typical student who uses this method:

> I already have the published copies [final drafts]. So...then I'll just rewrite the poems with a few little mistakes and I'll make it look like I edited it to what it is in the published copy. I'll fake it all, but that's okay.

Adolescents like Sarah who enjoy writing and are sufficiently marks driven may roll their eyes, but they agreeably engage in this subterfuge. For reluctant writers or less marks-oriented students, however, such manipulation of process and product is simply not worth the bother.

When teachers work with the actual processes that young writers use naturally, students can make great strides. Kelsey, for example, draws elaborate sketches of characters before he writes. The sketches help him to "flesh out" the characters he creates. When his teacher learned of these drawings, she accepted them as evidence of planning as indeed they were, in lieu of the assigned textual plan.

When students compose in multimedia environments, questions of process open up for reconsideration, to be worked out without the conventional orthodoxy of "planning sheet → draft → revision." However enshrined in classrooms, this process is simply not the way that many writers work. A fresh look at planning and revision processes is an invigorating exploration for teachers and can lead to a more flexible and open-ended approach to teaching planning and revision.

Composition in multimedia also lends itself easily to collaborative writing, which is increasingly required in workplaces. Discussing one multinational company's successful shift to a collaborative writing model, Williams and Marshall (1998) assert that "the individual writer is obsolete in the corporate world." Collaborative and multimedia work involves negotiations, decisions, and procedures different from those that authors may think of in connection to the composition of print text alone. As teachers work with students in composing in multimedia forms, they can position themselves next to, rather than in opposition to, their students and their real writing processes. Teachers reexamine and refresh their ideas about the process of writing and retune their teaching to better fit the actual processes of writers.

When adolescents compose in multimedia or hybrid forms, teachers may not be able to rely on traditional marking rubrics for evaluating the writing. When teachers highlight the question "What makes a good (comic book, webpage, etc.)?" they involve writers in the metacognitive work of setting evaluation criteria. When writers work in newer forms and media, or less studied forms, the question of what makes them good is still open to debate. In such discussions, teachers are sometimes surprised by their students' depth and understanding of forms that have not been taught in school. Writers learn more, and are galvanized to create more, from a discussion of the genuine intricacies of their work rather than from an evaluative mark.

With reluctant writers, the teacher's first order of business is to motivate them to write—often and on almost any subject. The threat of a mark or an exam will not inspire reluctant writers to buckle down and get their persuasive essays written. But, if teachers can encourage the students to get their ideas stated in some form, then they have a starting point. Teachers can open the discussion about how to present a particular work in another medium or form. If students learn techniques of organization, mood, tone, transitions, and suspense in film, for example, next they can learn how to craft these elements in print form. In this way, the written essay or narrative may be seen as one more form, and students can learn its conventions in comparison to those of other forms. (For an account of a project in which secondary students who were considered to be "at risk" and uncooperative wrote and published their own stories, see Britten, 2002.)

Conclusion

The challenge to match the literacy demands that students meet in school to the demands—and opportunities—that they meet in the world around them is a wide-reaching and exciting one. When teachers encourage adolescents to read and write in newer forms and media, to push boundaries with topics and forms, and to grapple with writing processes and the dilemmas of evaluation, they create school-based literacy opportunities that engage students in the genuine, rapidly changing, and sometimes contentious literacy world. In the shared enterprise of interpreting and engaging with contemporary literacy demands, teachers and students can work together to explore issues that have not yet been resolved in the broader world. This real-world challenge invigorates teaching and helps students see their teachers as literate adults rather than merely as authority figures. "Fun + complicated = work invested" in Aidan's implied formula is a useful starting point for teachers, too, for meeting this challenge with adolescent writers. It provides a way to untangle two knots of teaching at once.

NOTE: This chapter stems from research that has been supported by the Alberta Advisory Committee for Education Studies and by the Faculty of Education and Centre for Research on Literacy at the University of Alberta, Edmonton, Alberta, Canada, whose support I gratefully acknowledge.

REFERENCES

Atwell, N. (1998). *In the middle: New understandings about writing, reading, and learning.* Portsmouth, NH: Heinemann.

Britten, G. (2002). Loathe to write, love to be published. *The Secondary English Magazine, 6*(1), 17–20.

Dresang, E.T. (1999). *Radical change: Books for youth in a digital age.* New York: H.W. Wilson.

Eisner, E. (1997). Cognition and representation: A way to pursue the American dream? *Phi Delta Kappan, 78,* 349–353.

Ferreiro, E. (2000, Fall). Reading and writing in a changing world. *Publishing Research Quarterly,* 53–61.

Graves, D.H. (1994). *A fresh look at writing.* Portsmouth, NH: Heinemann.

Lewis, M. (2001, July). Faking it. *The New York Times Magazine, 44,* pp. 32–37.

Mackey, M., & McClay, J. (2000). Graphic routes to electronic literacy: Polysemy and picture books. *Changing English, 7*(2), 191–201.

McClay, J.K. (2002). Hidden "treasure": New genres, new media, and the teaching of writing. *English in Education, 36*(1), 43–52.

McCloud, S. (2000). *Reinventing comics: How imagination and technology are revolutionizing an art form.* New York: Perennial/HarperCollins.

New London Group. (1996). A pedagogy of multiliteracies: Designing social futures. *Harvard Education Review, 66*(1), 60–92.

Smith, M.W., & Wilhelm, J.D. (2002). *"Reading don't fix no Chevys": Literacy in the lives of young men.* Portsmouth, NH: Heinemann.

Tchudi, S., & Mitchell, D. (1999). *Exploring and teaching the English language arts* (4th ed.). Boston: Allyn & Bacon.

Wagner, R. (1996). Hyperstudio (Computer software). El Cajon, CA: Author.

Williams, N., & Marshall, C. (1998, August). *Global team rooms: New sites for multicultural discourse and documentation.* Paper presented at the National Council of Teachers of English "Global Conversations" Conference, Bordeaux, France.

Wright, R. (2001). *Hip and trivial: Youth culture, book publishing, and the greying of Canadian nationalism.* Toronto: Canadian Scholars Press.

LITERATURE CITED

Macaulay, D. (1990). *Black and white.* Boston: Houghton Mifflin.

Macaulay, D. (1995). *Shortcut.* Boston: Houghton Mifflin.

Myers, W.D. (1999). *Monster.* New York: HarperTempest.

Pilkey, D. (1997). *The adventures of Captain Underpants.* New York: The Blue Sky Press/Scholastic.

Walter, V. (1998). *Making up Megaboy.* New York: DK.

Wiesner, D. (2001). *The three pigs.* New York: Clarion Books.

Conclusions: Two Ways to Look at Knots

SHELLEY PETERSON

There are two ways to look at knots—either as tangles that need to be smoothed out or as ties that bring two or more things together in a helpful way. In this book, my fellow contributors and I looked at knots from both perspectives.

Some of us identified knots that we have been trying to untangle. These knots took a number of forms: adopting new approaches to teaching writing, teaching writing in a second language, teaching poetry, and examining taken-for-granted understandings about early writing processes and gendered assessment practices. Looking for ways to untangle the knots, we pulled apart and tugged at the snarls. We knitted in all that we had learned through reading the wealth of research and thinking available to us in published writing, as well as through our own experience and observations. In many cases, our untangling processes revealed new knots or variations on the tightly tangled knots that troubled us. We hoped that teachers reading of our struggles and successes would feel that they are not alone in their efforts to work through the inevitable knots of teaching writing.

Some writers in this book took the second approach to thinking about knots. We tied writing together with oral language, multiage groups, drama, popular culture, and technology to create knots that made writing an easier and more fulfilling process for students and for teachers. We gave many classroom examples of ways in which students in elementary and middle grades found renewed motivation and purpose for their writing when their teachers intermingled writing instruction with oral language, with various media, and with the arts. In one case, the use of computer technology created the types of knots that needed to be untangled, as students felt that they had lost the immediacy of conversations with their teacher while engaged in online dialogues. In the other chapters, however, intertwining writing with the arts, oral language, and popular culture created helpful knots, like those that sailors use to moor their boats to a dock. These intertwinings helped students and teachers to go beyond what they had imagined or expected to achieve.

Working with colleagues in creating this book has been an experience of discovering unimagined possibilities. We wish the same for our readers and their students—that some parts or all of this book may touch them in some way, so they may reach beyond what they had dreamed or anticipated was possible as writers and teachers of writers.

Author Index

A

Ackroyed, J., 109
Ada, A.F., 60
Alberta Education, 79
Alexander, L., 108
Alexander-Kasparik, R., 65
Allen, P., 69
Allwright, J.M., 67
Allwright, R.L., 67
Applebee, A.N., 79
Atwell, N., 1, 27, 98, 118

B

Baker, C., 66
Barnes, D., 1, 17
Barritt, L., 82
Barrs, M., 110, 114
Barthes, R., 101
Bayliss, V., 77
Beaumier, T., 7
Bell, M., 77
Biffignani, S., 88
Birkerts, S., 93
Blachman, B.A., 44
Bolton, G.M., 115
Booth, D., 109, 113, 114, 115
Bridwell, L.S., 25
Britten, G., 127
Britton, J., 17, 32
Brooks, L., 67
Bruner, J., 27, 47
Burnett, G., 89

C

Calkins, L.M., 7, 8, 10, 11, 88

Chang-Wells, G.L., 19
Clark, F., 82
Clay, M.M., 41, 47
Cloud, N., 52
Cohen, A.D., 61, 67
Cole, N., 79
Connors, K., 71, 72
Cork, V., 110, 114
Creech, S., 99
Cumming, A., 55
Cummins, J., 53, 54, 55, 56, 57, 59,
    61, 66, 69
Cunningham, A., 48

D

Dahl, K., 79
De Kerckhove, D., 100
Dewsbury, A., 91
Dresang, E.T., 119, 121, 124
Dyson, A.H., 40

E

Eisner, E., 119
Elbow, P., 101
Elwood, J., 79
Emig, J.A., 1
Esposito, N.G., 97, 98

F

Faigley, L., 25
Farnan, N., 79
Ferreiro, E., 47, 120, 121
Fletcher, R., 1
Freedman, S.W., 17

G

Gallagher, K., 109
Genesee, F., 52
Ghahremani-Ghajar, S., 56
Goodman, K., 82
Graves, D.H., 1, 7, 8, 10, 11, 13, 14,
    27, 48, 88, 109, 118
Gray-Schlegel, M., 77
Gray-Schlegel, T., 77

H

Haas, E., 60
Halliday, M.A.K., 19
Hamayan, E., 52
Harley, B., 69
Heaney, S., 96
Hornberger, N.H., 66
Hunter, J., 56
Huot, B., 83

J–K

Johnson, D.D., 79
Kobayashi, S., 59
Kowal, U.M., 74
Kress, G., 42, 43

L

Laminack, L.L., 1
Langer, J.A., 79
Lantolf, J.P., 75
Lapkin, S., 67, 68, 71
Leggo, C., 104
Lewis, M., 120, 125
Lindemann, E., 102
Lindfors, J.W., 19

M

Macaulay, D., 125

Mace-Matluck, B.J., 65
Mackey, M., 125
Mantello, M., 68
Marshall, C., 126
Masny, D., 56
McClay, J., 125
McCloud, S., 125
McCormick-Calkins, L., 1
Milosz, C., 96
Mitchell, D., 120
Morgan, K., 1
Mullis, I.V., 79
Murray, D., 1, 98
Myers, W.D., 125

N–O

Neelands, J., 109, 115
New London Group, 119
Ohio Department of Education, 79,
    80, 81
Olson, D., 41, 47
O'Malley, J.M., 52, 60, 63
Ord, J., 89
Oullette, B., 71, 72

P

Parsons, L., 98, 99
Pelletier, J., 40, 41, 42
Peterson, R., 25
Peterson, S., 10, 11, 77, 78
Peyton, J.K., 60
Phenix, J., 33
Phillips, L., 54
Pierce, L.V., 52, 60, 63
Pilkey, D., 122, 123
Poplin, M., 54
Power, B., 11
Purves, A., 82

Q

QI, D.S., 59
QUEEN, R.M., 65
QUINLAN, M., 79

R

REED, L., 60
RINNERT, C., 59
ROMATOWSKI, J.A., 77
ROSENBLATT, L., 82

S

SAKAMOTO, M., 56
SANGWINE, J., 61
SAYERS, D., 89
SCHMEICHEL, L., 74
SMITH, F., 93
SMITH, M.W., 119
STAKE, R., 29
STANOVICH, K., 40, 48
STANOVICH, P., 40, 48
STOBART, G., 79
STOCK, P.L., 82
STRENSKI, E., 97, 98
STUART, V., 98
SUDOL, D., 88
SUDOL, P., 88
SWAIN, M., 67, 68, 69, 70, 71

T

TANGEL, D.M., 44

TCHUDI, S., 120
TEBEROSKY, A., 47
THORNBURY, S., 74
TOLCHINSKY LANDSMAN, L., 41
TOMA, C., 27
TREPANIER-STREET, M.L., 77
TUCK, D., 77
TURBILL, J., 7

V–W

VERPLAETSE, L.S., 62
VYGOTSKY, L.S., 75
WAGNER, B., 109, 115
WAGNER, R., 118
WAJNRYB, R., 68
WALTER, V., 123
WEAVER, C., 66, 69, 74
WEINHOLD, K., 1
WELLS, G., 19, 27, 109
WERTSCH, J., 27
WESTERVELT, L., 88
WIESNER, D., 125
WILHELM, J.D., 119
WILLIAMS, N., 126
WITTE, S., 25
WODD RAY, K., 1
WOODLEY, M.P., 67
WRIGHT, R., 122
WYNNE-JONES, T., 23

Subject Index

Note: Page numbers followed by *f* indicate figures.

A

ACADEMIC LANGUAGE PROFICIENCY: of English language learners, 54

ADOLESCENT WRITERS: as mentors, 88–95 (*see also* online mentoring); reluctant, 118–128 (*see also* reluctant writers)

THE ADVENTURES OF CAPTAIN UNDERPANTS (PILKEY), 122

ANALYTIC RUBRICS: in assessment, 79–81, 82

APPROPRIATE LANGUAGE/TOPICS, 121–125

ASSESSMENT. *See* writing assessment

AUTHOR GROUPS: multiage, 28–39 (*see also* multiage author groups); in process approach, 13, 14

B

BABBLE AND DOODLE: in poetry writing, 104

C

CHILD STUDY APPROACH: for emergent writing, 47

CLASSROOM CONVERSATION. *See* peer conferences/discussions

CLASSROOM MANAGEMENT, 12

COLLABORATIVE DIALOGUE, 70–75

COMICS: for reluctant writers, 124–125

COMPUTERS. *See* online mentoring; technology

CONFERENCES: peer (*see* peer conferences/discussions); teacher-student, 9–10, 27–28, 62

CONTENT AREA WRITING: academic language proficiency and, 54; peer discussions for, 19, 21–22; process approach in, 12; reformulation in, 74–75; role-playing in, 21–22; in second language, 74–75

CONVERSATIONAL FLUENCY: of English language learners, 53–54

D

DIALOGUE JOURNALS: for English language learners, 60–61

DICTOGLOSS, 68–69

DISCRETE LANGUAGE SKILLS: of English language learners, 53–54

DOUBLE-VOICE POEMS, 105

DRAFT STAGE: in process approach, 8

DRAMA, 21–22, 108–117; as prewriting activity, 112; students' response to, 21–22, 108–117; writing after, 112–115. *See also* writing in role

DRAWINGS: in emergent writing, 11; by English language learners, 52–53, 54–55

E

EARLY PRINT UNDERSTANDING, 40–49; developmental differences in, 44–46, 45*f;* educational implications of, 46–49; examples of, 42–44, 43*f;* letter-like forms in, 43–46, 43*f;* numerical notation in, 43–46, 43*f;* referential writing and, 42–44, 43*f,* 48; research in, 41–46; scribble writing and, 42–43. *See also* emergent writing

EDITING: in process approach, 8

ELECTRONIC NETWORKING, 88–95. *See also* online mentoring

EMERGENT WRITING: child study approach for, 47; conceptions of print in, 40–49 (*see also* early print understanding); drawings in, 11; encouragement of, 48–49; family involvement in, 43; holistic approach for, 48–49; learning by construction and, 43; learning by imitation and, 43, 47; learning by instruction and, 43; letter-like forms in, 43–46, 43*f;* numerical notation in, 43–46, 43*f;* referential vs. phonetic, 48; topic ideas for, 49

ENGLISH LANGUAGE LEARNERS: classroom publication projects for, 62; dialogue journals for, 60–61; drawing and labeling by, 52–53, 54–55; extra help for, 57, 58, 62; instructional approaches for, 57–64; language proficiency of, 53–54; learning disabilities in, 54, 58; mainstreaming of, 52–53, 57–58; needs assessment for, 58–59; nonteacher assistance for, 59–60; peer assistance for, 59–60; reformulation by, 61, 66–75 (*see also* reformulation); sociocultural issues and, 56–57; use of first language by, 55, 59–60; writing assessment for, 62–63

F

FAMILY INVOLVEMENT: in emergent writing, 47; in multiage author groups, 37

FREEWRITING, 101–102

FUNCTIONAL ILLITERACY, 120

G

GENDER EXPECTATIONS, 78–85; assessment and, 80–85; awareness of, 82, 84–85; gender stereotypes and, 78–79; instructional implications of, 84–85

GRAMMAR: vocabulary and, 69–70
GRAPHIC NOVELS: for reluctant writers, 124–125

H

HERE AND NOW LITERACY, 120
HIGH SCHOOL STUDENTS: as mentors, 38, 89–95 (*see also* online mentoring);
    as reluctant writers, 118–127
HOLISTIC SCORING: in assessment, 80–82

I

ILLUSTRATED BOOKS: for reluctant writers, 124–125
IMITATIVE LEARNING, 43, 47
IMMERSION PROGRAMS. *See* English language learners
INTERNET. *See* online mentoring; technology

J

JOURNALS: dialogue, 60–61; online mentoring and, 90–91

K

THE KIDS FROM KANATA PROJECT, 89
KNOT METAPHOR, 2, 129–130

L

LABELING: by English language learners, 52–53, 54–55
LANGUAGE: appropriate, 121–125; performative aspects of, 100–101
LANGUAGE PROFICIENCY: academic, 54; conversational, 53–54
LANGUAGE-RELATED EPISODES, 70–71
LEARNING: by construction, 43; by imitation, 43, 47; by instruction, 43;
    student-centered vs. teacher-controlled, 7
LETTER-LIKE FORMS: in emergent writing, 43–46, 43*f*
LETTERS TO THE EDITOR, 21

M

MAINSTREAMING: of English language learners, 52–53, 57–58
MAKING UP MEGABOY (WALTER), 123–124
MENTORS: older students as, 38, 89–95; online, 89–95. *See also* online
    mentoring
MODELING: for English language learners, 60; in process approach, 14
MULTIAGE AUTHOR GROUPS, 29–39; adult participation in, 37, 38; agenda for,
    29–30, 30*f*, 32*f*, 34*f*–36*f*; brainstorming in, 30–32; collective energy

in, 33–34; for family writing, 37; functions of, 33; older students' participation in, 38; participant satisfaction with, 37–39; revision process in, 32–36; shared opportunities in, 35; success of, 38; supportive nature of, 33, 34, 36

N

NEWSPAPER ARTICLES: student-written, 21; as topic source, 20
NUMERICAL NOTATION: in emergent writing, 43–46, 43*f*

O

OLDER STUDENTS: as mentors, 38, 89–95 (*see also* online mentoring); as reluctant writers, 118–127
ONLINE MENTORING, 88–95; anonymity in, 92, 94; classroom dynamics and, 90–91; results of, 92–94; writing journals and, 90–91
ORAL LANGUAGE: in writing instruction, 17–26
ORILLAS PROJECT, 89

P

PEER ASSISTANCE: for English language learners, 59–60
PEER CONFERENCES/DISCUSSIONS, 19–26, 27; in author groups, 13, 14, 27–39 (*see also* author groups); in content area instruction, 19, 21–22; effectiveness of, 19, 23–26; encouraging participation in, 19–20; examples of, 23–25; negative feedback in, 25–26; in process approach, 14; about published literature, 23; revision and, 18–19, 23–25; about student writing, 18, 23–25; value of, 23–26
PHONETIC WRITING, 48
PING PONG ACTIVITY, 103–104
POETRY, 96–106; barriers to writing/appreciating, 98–99; double-voice, 105; freewriting for, 101–102; misconceptions about, 97–98; nurturing writers of, 100–105; rhyme in, 104–105; topics for, 103–104; word play in, 102–105
POLYSEMIC CODES, 125
POPULAR CULTURE: use of, 119–124
PREWRITING/REHEARSAL: in process approach, 7
PRIMARY TRAIT SCORING, 80, 81–82
PRINT: children's conceptions of, 40–49. *See also* early print understanding
PROCESS APPROACH. *See* writing process model
PROJECT HEADLIGHT, 89
PUBLISHING: by English language learners, 62; in process approach, 8, 13

R

REFERENTIAL WRITING, 42–44, 43*f*, 48

REFORMULATION, 61, 66–75; collaborative nature of, 67, 70–75; definition of, 67; examples of, 69–73; language-related episodes in, 70–71; task stages in, 67–73, 69*f*; vs. text reconstruction, 67

RELUCTANT WRITERS, 11–12, 118–127; appropriate language/topics and, 119–124; boundary pushing by, 121–125; collaborative approach for, 126; here and now literacy and, 120; illustrated books for, 124–125; motivational strategies for, 126–127; multimedia approach for, 120–121, 125–127; technology applications for, 119–121; writing process for, 125–127

REVISION: peer conferences and, 18–19, 23–25; in process approach, 8, 14–15

ROLE-PLAYING, 21–22, 108–117. *See also* writing in role

S

SECOND LANGUAGE LEARNING: content area instruction in, 74–75; reformulation in, 61, 66–75. *See also* English language learners

SPELLING, 10

STEREOTYPES: gender, 78–79. *See also* gender expectations

STUDENT-CENTERED TEACHING, 7

T

TALKING: in writing instruction, 17–26

TEACHER-STUDENT CONFERENCES: for English language learners, 62; in process approach, 9–10

TECHNOLOGY: for emergent writers, 49; integration of, 119–120; in online mentoring, 88–95. *See also* online mentoring

TEXT RECONSTRUCTION, 67. *See also* reformulation

TIME CONSTRAINTS: technology and, 88–95

TOPIC IDEAS, 10, 13; appropriateness of, 121–125; for emergent writers, 49; newspaper articles and, 20–21; for poems, 103–104; sources of, 10

V

VOCABULARY: grammar and, 69–70

W

WANDER FOR WONDER ACTIVITY, 103

WRITERS IN ELECTRONIC RESIDENCE (WIER), 89, 94

WRITING: content area (*see* content area writing); as creative activity, 101; emergent (*see* emergent writing); referential, 42–44, 43*f*, 48

WRITING ASSESSMENT: analytic rubrics for, 79–81; analytic rubrics in, 79–81, 82; for English language learners, 62–63; gender issues in, 77–85; holistic scoring in, 80–82; primary trait scoring in, 80–82; subjectivity in, 82–83

WRITING BUDDIES, 9, 11

WRITING CONFERENCES: peer (*see* peer conferences/discussions); teacher-student, 9–10

WRITING IN ROLE, 21–22, 112–117; benefits of, 115–116; after drama experience, 112–115; as empathetic activity, 116; prewriting activities and, 112; as reflective activity, 115; remembered roles and, 114–115; as social activity, 116; students' responses to, 117

WRITING INSTRUCTION: appropriate language/topics and, 121–125; drama in, 108–117; for English language learners, 52–64; freewriting in, 101–102; gender issues in, 77–85; poetry in, 96–106; process approach to, 7–16; for reluctant adolescents, 118–128; role-playing in, 21–22, 108–117; in second language, 66–75; traditional approach to, 6–7

WRITING JOURNALS: for English language learners, 60–61; online mentoring and, 90–91

WRITING PROCESS MODEL, 7–16; advantages of, 15–16; author groups in, 13, 14; classroom management and, 12; in content area writing, 12; editing stage in, 8; modeling in, 14; peer conferences in, 14; prewriting/rehearsal stage in, 7; publishing stage in, 8, 13; for reluctant writers, 11–12, 118–119, 125–127; revision stage in, 8, 14–15; teacher's experience with, 8–16; teacher-student conferences in, 11–12; writing buddies in, 9, 11; writing (draft) stage in, 8

WWF COMPETITION, 103